Contesting Masculinities and Women's Agency in Kashmir

MEN AND MASCULINITIES IN A TRANSNATIONAL WORLD

Series Editors: Simona Sharoni (SUNY Plattsburgh) and Henri Myrttinen (International Alert)

In the past two decades, the field of men and masculinities studies has been steadily growing in both breadth and depth. As a result, working with men and masculinities has gained increased interest not only among scholars in the academy but also among policy makers and practitioners. This is reflected in a steady increase in research on masculinities but also in the growth of the global MenEngage movement. In the political arena, the recent UN Security Council Resolution 2242 on gender, peace, and security also specifically mentioned working with men and boys. At the same time, however, critical men and masculinities studies remain underrepresented in research and policy debates, as well as in academic publications and curricula. The book series aims to advance interdisciplinary/multidisciplinary/transdisciplinary scholarship on men and masculinities.

Titles in the Series

Contesting Masculinities and Women's Agency in Kashmir

Amya Agarwal

ROWMAN & LITTLEFIELD
Lanham • Boulder • New York • London

Published by Rowman & Littlefield
An imprint of The Rowman & Littlefield Publishing Group, Inc.
4501 Forbes Boulevard, Suite 200, Lanham, Maryland 20706
www.rowman.com

86-90 Paul Street, London EC2A 4NE

British Library Cataloguing in Publication Information Available

Library of Congress Cataloging-in-Publication Data

Names: Agarwal, Amya, author.
Title: Contesting masculinities and women's agency in Kashmir / Amya Agarwal.
Description: Lanham: The Rowman & Littlefield Publishing Group, Inc., | Series: Men
    and masculinities in a transnational world |
Includes bibliographical references and index. | Summary: "Based on rich empirical data,
    this book explores the politics of competing and sometimes overlapping masculinities
    represented in the Kashmir valley. It broadens the understanding of women's
    agency through its engagement with the construction, performance and interplay of
    masculinities in conflict."—Provided by publisher.
Identifiers: LCCN 2022001239 (print) | LCCN 2022001240 (ebook) |
    ISBN 9781786612397 (cloth) | ISBN 9781538198780 (paper) | ISBN
    9781786612403 (epub)
Subjects: LCSH: Men—India—Jammu and Kashmir—Psychology. | Masculinity—
    India—Jammu and Kashmir—History. | Masculinity—Social aspects—India—Jammu
    and Kashmir. | Sex role—India—Jammu and Kashmir—History.
Classification: LCC HQ1090.7.I4 A43 2022 (print) | LCC HQ1090.7.I4 (ebook) | DDC
    305.310954/63—dc23/eng/20220228
LC record available at https://lccn.loc.gov/2022001239
LC ebook record available at https://lccn.loc.gov/2022001240

For my interviewees, interlocutors, and friends in Kashmir—
for their time, help and support in the field research.
For single parents and children of single parents—striving to make
a place for themselves in sometimes an alienating world.

For my grandfather, "Nanan" (1930–2014), from whom I
learned early lessons on care and unconditional love.
For my daughter, "Amaira," who brings happiness,
light, and joy in my life every day.

Contents

Acknowledgments

This book was written and revised during my postdoctoral research fellowship at the Centre for Global Cooperation Research, Duisburg, Germany. I extend my gratitude to Sigrid Quack, Matthias Schuller, and Freya Köhler for providing suitable research, administrative and office support. I am most grateful to my colleagues, Katja Freistein and Christine Unrau, for their sustained encouragement and friendship. My former officemate, Zeynep Sahin Mencutek, provided generous suggestions, guidance, and also shared my care work on important days. In many ways, she became my family in Duisburg. My special thanks to her.

My current institutional home, Arnold-Bergstraesser-Institut, University of Freiburg, provided strong support during the book production stage. I thank the entire research team, and in particular, Franzisca Zanker, Helga Dickow, and Clemens Jürgenmeyer for the gift of their friendship, kindness, and warmth that I cherish most in the beautiful city of Freiburg. Many thanks also to Arne Bode and Frederik Hermle for their close reading of the proofs and their helpful suggestions.

No words can express my gratitude to the book series editor, Henri Myrttinen, who patiently went through several rounds of drafts and provided detailed comments, which not only helped in making considerable improvements to the book, but also became a great learning opportunity for me. He accompanied the manuscript throughout and held my words and thoughts with so much care. Thank you, Henri.I also thank the Rowman & Littlefield (R&L) publishing team, especially Katelyn Turner and Michael Hals for their understanding during the book production. Dhara Snowden was the senior commissioning editor when I first discussed the book idea in Baltimore, 2017, and I thank her for believing in my work.

The research in this book was part of my PhD thesis, and I am thankful to my supervisor, Navnita C. Behera for encouraging me to strive for better and making me understand the value of hard-work. I also owe thanks to my fellow PhD course-mates for their encouragement. My friends and research interlocutors in Kashmir provided steadfast support for conducting field research in several districts, and I thank them for their time and tireless efforts. I extend my gratitude to each interviewee who trusted me enough to share their lived experiences. Despite the short encounters, their caring ways and conversations have stayed with me. Many thanks to professors in different universities in Kashmir for generously sharing their research experiences that helped me gain valuable insights into the Kashmiri society and culture. I also thank employees at various governmental and non-governmental organizations in Kashmir for promptly providing relevant data.

I was fortunate to have found academic camaraderie and inspiration during the book-writing process. Philipp Schulz, Heleen Touquet, Roxani Krystalli, Swati Parashar, David Duriesmith and Shweta Singh are some academics whose work, patience, and kindness have greatly influenced my thoughts and writing. My former colleagues, and dear friends in Delhi—Sandhya Devesan Nambiar, Renny Thomas, Jessy Phillip, and Roshan Xalxo provided academic guidance and emotional support through the process: debates, discussions, carrom, food explorations, shared love for *dhaba* chai, and sometimes nightlong conversations on gender—all helped in the articulation of some of the initial ideas in the book. I am grateful to them. I also thank my students at University of Delhi and South Asian University for their important reflections and engaging conversations.

Material collected during my PhD research in Kashmir was also used to write other articles, book chapters and blogs. The information was carefully employed to avoid major overlaps with the content in the book. In addition, my own ways of thinking, of analysis and of articulation have undergone significant changes since I wrote the previous pieces. Acknowledging the evolving process of thinking and writing is also an important part of the academic journey.

This book was written during a challenging period of my life, marked with a few transitions. For the same, I convey thanks to my family, especially to my maternal grandmother for her unconditional love; and to my mother and maternal uncle for their faith and encouragement. The strength to complete this book as a single mother (during a global pandemic and in a foreign country) is a legacy I received in unconscious ways from my own (single) mother. Sorry that it took a whole pandemic for me to realize this—thank you, ma. As I finalize the book proofs at my maternal grandparents' house in Bhopal, I am beginning to value how this home has provided a sense of roots and security in my life. Returning to the feeling of home has been both a restoring and healing experience.

Some friendships are blessings that make difficult times seem tolerable. I thank Nidhi Sharma Parashar and Sophia De for their strong support in hard times. Their wholehearted acceptance and generosity fills my heart with gratitude and love. I also thank Vineet Thakur for being there in these trying times. My heartfelt thanks to Kavita Didi for taking care of my daughter during the long fieldwork hours and so much more. Her caring presence has been a huge blessing in our lives.

Finally, my deepest gratitude to my daughter, Amaira, who has been my companion at each step of the making of this book: starting from field research in Kashmir as an eight-month-old baby to traveling across continents as an eight-year-old and now to providing expert advice on handling pressures. Her patience, acceptance, and love for me—in this process and beyond—make all the challenges seem worthwhile. Thank you, Amaira.

Chapter 1

Gender, Agency, and Field Research Experiences in Conflict

Various explorations have been carried out by feminist scholars to understand the significance of gender in conflict zones. The construction of gender roles, identities, and expectations along with their influence in conflicts are widely discussed as part of this endeavor. These discussions, however, have a tendency to focus mainly on the perspectives of women. The available literature on gender in conflicts majorly involves the study of women's roles, participation, and struggles. Documenting the active role of women in conflicts is, no doubt, an important exercise to make visible and give voice to women's experiences. However, an equally significant part—how gender influences men and masculinities—often gets somewhat overlooked in the process. Having said that, it is also important to recognize that several attempts are already made to fill this gap. Critical masculinities studies offers a rich account of how gender influences men in different conflict and postconflict contexts (both in the "Global North and South"). The work of Raewyn Connell, Brandon Hamber, Henri Myrttinen, Christine Beasley, Claire Duncanson, GuÐrún Sif FriÐriksdóttir, and Kimberly Theidon, and the more recent empirical studies conducted by Élise Féron, David Duriesmith, Maria Eriksson Baaz, Maria Stern, Heleen Touquet, Janine Clark, and Philipp Schulz are few examples in this direction.[1]

Using a detailed ethnographic study conducted in the Kashmir valley between 2013 and 2016, this book attempts to combine the elements of both critical masculinities' studies and feminist research. In doing so, the book argues that in order to arrive at a meaningful understanding of women's (and men's) agency in conflict situations, an in-depth engagement with existing multiple masculinities is required. Furthermore, the study of women's choices, roles, and perspectives remains incomplete without studying the politics of masculinities in conflict. This is because the context in which women exercise their choices and perform practices is shaped and informed by an interplay of multiple masculinities. The book uncovers, on the one hand, a significant contestation found in the "mosaic of masculinities"[2] in the Kashmir conflict; and on the other hand, analyses how agency in conflict is engaged with these multiple, contesting, and often paradoxical masculinities. The title, *Contesting Masculinities*, is not a provocation but an invitation to understand the practices and interplay of masculinities in conflict situations. Here, it may be important to mention that the study entailed in this book is not intended to merely focus on the gender politics of Kashmir but rather develop our understanding of masculinities and agency through the context of Kashmir. In other words, the book highlights what the local dynamics in Kashmir society can contribute towards the universal study of men and masculinities in conflicts in a transnational world.

The ongoing conflict in Kashmir is predominantly viewed, reported, and discussed from a state lens, especially in the mainstream platforms. The states in question—India and Pakistan—and their antagonistic relations have shaped much of the existing discourse around the conflict. This is also visible in the discussions found within the traditional international relations (IR) discipline. This book moves beyond the disciplinary bounds and adopts a trans-disciplinary approach to understanding the gender dimension of the Kashmir conflict. This is because feminist, sociological, anthropological, and ethnographical inquiries have better addressed the gaps in the state-centric version of the conflict and highlighted the multiplicity of stakeholders in Kashmir in a more nuanced way, as compared to their traditional IR counterparts. In the same light, this book derives huge inspiration from these non-mainstream accounts, especially feminist research.

Existing feminist literature on the Kashmir conflict entails extensive empirical research on the diverse ways of women's participation in the resistance. I think it is an incorrect assumption that feminist scholarship on Kashmir has mainly focused on the experiences and victimization of women. The previous oversimplification of women's agency within water-tight binaries and frameworks of victimhood and agents is now extensively challenged. Contemporary feminist research has gone beyond the monolithic and stereotypical discourses on victimization and activism, to understand the complexities of women's agency. Parashar's work is a suitable example that touches upon the nuances of women's everyday lived choices in conflict:

> The paradoxes in the lives of women involved in the religio-political militant projects cannot be entirely captured by uncomplicated theoretical frameworks of agency and empowerment. (Parashar, 2014)

Similarly, Malik's detailed exploration of Muslim women's agency in the Kashmiri resistance provides a powerful critique of the postcolonial feminist literature for its lack of a critical understanding of the lives of Muslim women in Kashmir.

> Much of the conventional feminist scholarship on Kashmir has merely reproduced the dominant narrative of Muslim women being either voiceless victims, or ideological supporters of men. (Malik, 2019)

Building upon both Parashar's assessment of women's creative and complex negotiation of spaces and Malik's emphasis on the Muslim identity and performance of women as "acts of self-formation and struggles against oppressive subjection"—this book attempts to extend the complex understanding of women's agency through its engagement with masculinities. The complexities that shape the agency of women in Kashmir cannot be studied in isolation from the interplay of masculinities. How women perceive their reality and make choices is not disconnected from the ecosystem of gender performativity in which men and masculinities also play an integral part. The myriad ways in which women make choices have a dialectical relationship with the masculinities in conflict.

So far, there is a limited exploration of masculinities in the Kashmir conflict. This also explains the absence of a theoretical anchor from within the context. As a result, this book relies on the theoretical parameters of masculinities developed in other conflict and postconflict contexts, along with the empirical observations and field research in Kashmir. The competitive masculinities of the state armed forces and the militant groups, masculinity associated with the religion, conflict affected civilian masculinities, and other nonmilitarized forms of masculinity represented by the human rights activists all form a web of masculinities in Kashmir. The book aims to uncover and further complicate women's agency through its engagement with this web, mainly with the interplay of militarized masculinities represented by both state and non-state actors. The interjection of the masculinities discourse can also be seen as an innovative attempt to revisit and reimagine the gender approach to studying the Kashmir conflict.

Before going further, it may be useful to lay down the meaning attached to the term *agency* in this book. Agency is most commonly defined as the ability to formally "act" in the "public" or "political" sphere not in isolation but rather in relation to the social world. Over a period of time, feminist scholarship has critically engaged with the limited understanding of agency that is not only based on the problematic binary of "public" and "private" but is also associated with the gendered division of labor that marginalizes women. In this regard, feminist scholars broaden the notion of agency by including intersubjective experiences and choices of women. Keeping the relational aspect of agency in mind, Judith Butler's (1999) idea of gender performativity is particularly relevant, which calls our attention on the performative mode of gender in addition to its social construction. In this reading, gender identities are perceived and performed (in relation to others) as a "mode of belief" both for self-building and against oppression and marginalization.

Feminist scholars have further added nuance by highlighting the gendered representations and frames to limit or restrict women's agency. Sjoberg and Gentry's (2007) work is significant in this regard, as they elaborate on the "mother," "monster," and "whore" narratives often used to denote instances of women's violence as exceptions. By reducing violence of women as singular, exceptional, and freak accidents, such narratives help in reinforcing the norms of typical female behavior and the images of "normal" women as peaceful remain intact. "Flawed femininity" is often blamed for women's transgressions. Instead of viewing women's engagement in violence as a deliberate choice or a reference to the sociopolitical context in which those choices are made, these narratives attribute their violence to a problem in their biological makeup and denies their capacity to make an independent choice.

More recent feminist interventions highlight the multiple complexities that shape agency. Björkdahl and Selimovic (2015) have rightly identified three central components of women's agency in existing feminist research: transformative, critical, and creative. The defining point of transformative agency is "the achievement of change, whereas action presumes no such transformation" (Shepherd, 2011). The critical agency in the words of McNay (2000) "refers to a critical disposition against the status quo and a commitment to social change based on a fundamental rethinking of gendered relationships." Creative agency moves beyond the conventional understanding of agency to include novel ways in which women negotiate and reappropriate everyday spaces. Parashar (2014), in her research on Kashmir and Sri Lanka, insists upon acknowledging the creative ways in which women claim their space in conflict settings. Here she refers to Bucar's (2011) concept of creative conformity that comprises "actions that may not produce ends that appear feminist within a secular-liberal framework, nor necessarily align with the intentions of the agent, but nonetheless influence gendered norms about the moral life."

The agential aspect dealt in this work is mostly inspired by the analysis of agency provided by critical feminist inquiry in IR as discussed above. In the context of Kashmir, recent contemplation around the complex idea of agency moves beyond studying only women's activism against human rights violations and oppressive subjection to understand their performed choices in accordance with their perceived identity. However, agency is not constituted by, or restricted to, a single gender identity and its performative roles. In this respect, the book also explores agency through ways in which men navigate gender expectations, perform acts and make choices to rebuild their selves; and confront their gender identity crisis. Taking inspiration from the illustrious work of Schulz and Touquet (2020) on creative agency of male survivors of sexual violence in both Ugandan and Croatian contexts, I attempt to look at both "silence" and "voice" as significant ways in which men use their agency in Kashmir. Exercising agency thus, as demonstrated in the book, includes the innumerable ways in which both men and women make choices in order to make sense of themselves and to negotiate space in their everyday lived experiences of conflict. As Saba Mahmood (2001) aptly puts it, agency should be understood not simply as "a synonym for resistance to relations of dominance, but as a capacity for action that specific relations of subordination create and enable."

Methodology, Data Collection, and Ethics

This book is based on extensive ethnographic research undertaken between 2013 and 2016 in the Kashmir valley. It includes interviews of multiple actors and stakeholders in the Kashmir conflict from various districts in the valley: Budgam, Anantnag, Shopian, Palwama, Baramulla, Kupwara, and Srinagar. The interviews were conducted with eighteen ex-militants, twelve surrendered militants; eleven young boys, and one girl who were involved in the stone-pelting movement of 2008 and 2010; and sixteen men employed (or retired) in the state armed forces. It also includes thirty-four interviews of mothers of killed militants/of ex-militants/of surrendered militants/of young boys killed after stone-pelting movement/and of young boys with pellet injuries. Ten interviews with women elected representatives (*panch* and *sarpanch*) of village halqas (local self-governing bodies), eight half-widows, and seven widows. Ten interviews (five male and five female) with those working in NGOs and human rights organization were also conducted. Alongside, I also interviewed nine public figures in the Kashmiri resistance. The names of all interviewees are anonymized/changed to protect their identities. The interviews were facilitated by my basic knowledge of Urdu. For those respondents who spoke only in Kashmiri, my research collaborator, Abid (name changed), acted as a translator. The reason for interviewing a diverse group of stakeholders was, first, to broaden the understanding of the Kashmir conflict as not just centered between states but through the perspectives of multiple stakeholders; second, to understand how the gender identities are constructed and reinforced in conflict and resistance. The interviewees were selected on a random basis from the lists of actors received from the government, NGOs and human rights groups. Sometimes, the respondents were selected through leads provided by the previous respondents, people in the villages, and friends working in NGOs in Srinagar.

Qualitative research tools in the form of interviews, oral testimonies, narratives were used extensively in the research. Along with these, visual and audio sources such as graffiti, slogans, photographs, engravings, poetry on graves, folk songs, songs sung in political rallies and funeral processions, and speeches in mosques, among others, are used as significant tools to understand embedded practices to reinforce gender. The narratives and testimonies collected are mainly in Urdu language and in many places the original idioms and phrases are cited in order to let the authenticity of the experience remain. The research also attends to the "meta-data," explained by Fujii (2010) as informants' spoken and unspoken thoughts and feelings which they do not always articulate in their stories or interview responses, but which emerge in other ways. In line with Fujii's analysis of the five types of meta-data—rumors, inventions, denials, evasions, and silences—the field research entailed in this book also includes a careful observation of the surroundings, the rumors, body language, the emotional reactions, evasions, and silences to understand the memories and experiences of the respondents. Participant observation is also an extremely important method, which was used to make the interviewees feel more comfortable. The respondents were very kind to involve me in their daily activities such as apple picking, farming, preparing meals, and sharing food in single-plate meals. The book borrows from feminist research methodology and goes beyond the so-called objective and scientific ways of doing research. In doing so, it avoids restricting research to the academic standard of argumentation and instead allows the field to speak through the pages. Some of the existing feminist literature on Kashmir use innovative writing styles that capture the emotions and nuances of everyday life in conflict. This book also takes inspiration from such work like that of Urvashi Bhutalia (2002), Swati Parashar (2014), Seema Kazi (2009), among others.

Some of the data was collected from government offices such as Human Rights Commission and police records of domestic violence. Reports and documentation of human rights violation was collected from NGOs and human rights groups. NGOs, such as Jammu & Kashmir Coalition of Civil Society (JKCCS), Association of Parents of Disappeared Persons (APDP), and also Muslim Khawateen Markaz (MKM) were extremely helpful and shared vast material of human rights abuses. I also went to University of Kashmir and the Islamic University of Science and Technology for collecting information on social aspects of the Kashmiri society. A professor of sociology at the University of Kashmir was very kind to give time to explain his research on women's position in Kashmir. I am also very grateful to the professors from department of Arabic studies in the Islamic University who took out time to explain different interpretations of Islam and provided material for the same. After the interview with a popular separatist leader, I was gifted a beautiful copy of the Quran, and whatever may be his motivation in doing so, I must say that it was a very useful companion in my preliminary research on understanding the masculine aspects of different Islamic interpretations. Textual analysis is also a significant part of the research, since a number of state and nonstate groups issued their pamphlets, books, and reports with relevant and useful information for the research.

The idea of ethics in this research is in line with few parameters previously developed by scholars conducting field research in conflict and other politically sensitive contexts. The study adopts a "do no harm" ethical imperative, which is in accordance with E. J. Wood's (2006) understanding of informed consent of the respondents toward the research project, to protect the politically sensitive data and to decide what material to publish. Oral consent procedures were used where the respondents were thoroughly explained the purpose of the research and the significance of their response. The primary aim being the protection of the participants in the research so that they do not run risks as a result of their participation. In doing so, I have adopted an anonymity and confidentiality approach, where I either change the names of those interviewed or keep them anonymous. Also, I kept the material gathered as confidential as possible. Second, taking inspiration from feminist research ethics, this body of work follows a consistent interrogation of "epistemic oppression" (Ackerly, Friedman, Menon, and Zalewski, 2020) especially in field research. One example is the use of decolonial ethnography in which the vocabulary is used with particular care. The use of the phrase "subject," for instance, comes with colonial connotations. Hence, this study adopts terms such as "respondents," "research partners," "collaborators," or "interlocutors" to highlight the co-constructive and mutual aspects in the process of knowledge production. Also, the names and identities of the translators, helpers, and friends have been changed or made anonymous for their protection.

The pursued research reflects an attempt to foreground the local experiences of global politics.

The field work in Kashmir was not free of ethical dilemmas and emotional challenges. As previously mentioned, the protection of respondents was a concern through-out the research. This involved questions around data security and documentation. For instance, I took decisions such as not recording interviews of the locals (except for some public figures who were vocal about their position) as that could put them in a vulnerable position. Every time I left Srinagar, my laptop and pen drives were checked at the airport security, or when my material was checked at sensitive areas in other districts of the valley, it also meant risking the protection of the respondents who had trusted me enough to share their past experiences, information, and material. While I was in constant touch with my supervisor and closely followed the ethical guidelines of the university, still I felt immense responsibility and concern toward the responses of my respondents.

For some time (around two years) after the submission of my PhD thesis, it was challenging to write a full research paper or publish anything substantial, as there was guilt attached in publishing the stories and almost felt like an extractive and exploitative exercise. I was deeply concerned about my incapacity as an author and the incommensurability of language to do justice to the profound painful experiences shared by some of my interviewees. Whenever I wrote something, I felt that a lot got lost in translation. At one point, I contemplated submitting my findings to responsible NGOs, who could do something about the concerns and issues of the concerned people. It was only later in 2017 when I attended presentations of people doing similar work in sensitive areas with resonating emotional and ethical challenges, that I decided to publish this work. I am grateful that I got a chance to learn about the work of scholars studying masculinities discourse in different conflict settings. Especially at the ISA convention in Baltimore, I was fortunate that the book series editor, Henri Myrttinen, encouraged me to learn from different panels on masculinities in conflict and postconflict contexts.

The time period from the start of the field work to the completion of this book is marked by several changes in the political atmosphere of Kashmir. From the perspective of the methodological challenges, some activists and interviewees who were interviewed during the field research and had given approval for quoting their names underwent detentions and raids; some had no internet connectivity or even passed away; consequently, it was impossible to seek fresh approvals for the book. As a result, and as previously mentioned, I have anonymized their names or changed their identity. The reason I state this is to highlight that changing political circumstances of a conflict-affected society have a direct impact on interviewees and the research as a whole. Reflecting on how such changes affect the interviewees and finding the most ethical solution to publish research can be challenging but is required of a researcher to reflect on. For methodological transparency, in the following section I discuss some reflections on my positionality and the answer to the most important question in field research—how did I gain access to the field?

Reflections of Field Research and Positionality

Keeping in mind the sensitivity of conducting research in Kashmir, it is important to reflect honestly on my motivations, positionality and background—and their implications on conducting research in Kashmir. As a first step, I provide the answer to a question all field researchers must state transparently—How did I gain access to the field? In 2013, I was recruited as one of the field researchers for a project on conflict governance headed by my PhD supervisor. As part of this project, field researchers from Delhi were teamed up with Kashmiri researchers. The field researchers (from both Delhi and Kashmir) were students of Masters,' MPhil and PhD. My research partner was a Kashmiri student, Abid, who became a close friend, advisor and guide. From an academic level perspective, he was 'junior' to me, but had immense experience of conducting field research in different districts of Kashmir. After our project-related field trip was over, we remained in touch along with a few other Kashmiri researchers. After many discussions on my PhD topic, they very generously offered to help me with my PhD field research.

I made several trips to Kashmir between 2013 and 2016; and Abid (with the help of his friends and teachers) meticulously arranged interviews with various stakeholders for each trip. We hired a driver who drove us to several districts tirelessly without charging much and also became a good friend later. I am so grateful for his kindness and friendship. As already mentioned, Abid accompanied me for each interview and also helped translate the interviews. My PhD field research was funded partly by the University teaching assis-tantship scholarship that I received from 2010 to 2014; and money borrowed from my mother. The interviews with all the mentioned interviewees were arranged with the help of my friends and Kashmiri interlocutors, and there was no involvement of the Indian government, my University or my PhD supervisor in arranging these interviews. Some army personnel employed in Kashmir were asked for an interview promptly during the fieldwork and they agreed to talk. Some retired army officers and those who had worked previously in Kashmir, were contacted through friends. The purpose of my research was clearly explained to all the participants, and I am very grateful to them for their time, effort and trust in me. Their consent was central in the pursuit of the research.

In the process of conducting field research in Kashmir, I have learned that as an "outsider" researcher, it is so important to constantly reflect upon the positionality and impact of one's research on the interviewees and their families. For a researcher, their research is usually driven by curiosity and passion; however, the research process could have dire consequences for the research participants. A recent case of an anthropological research in Kashmir triggered a debate around the ethics of field research. Keeping such debates in mind, I find it imperative to also state a few lines about my background and my motivation to conduct this research.

I belong to an upper-caste Hindu family. I was raised by a single mother with the support of my maternal grandparents in Bhopal, the capital city of Madhya Pradesh state in India. I have not known my biological or stepfa-ther's family, so I only speak of my maternal family. After completing school, I moved to Delhi in 2003 for higher studies. I completed my graduation, post-graduation and MPhil from the University of Delhi and was pursuing

my PhD at the time of the fieldwork. During my PhD research I was married
and living in Gurgaon. Neither my family nor my ex-husband's family had
any direct association with politics in Kashmir. My interest in the gender
dimension of the Kashmir conflict was an extension of my MPhil research
on women's peacebuilding efforts in the conflict settings of Northeast India,
and initially I wanted to pursue a comparative study of these contexts. Here,
I must also clearly state that the point of this study is not to take sides in the
conflict, but to understand how studying gender and masculinities can provide alternative ways of questioning the complex power relations and open
avenues for more people-centric and empathetic approaches to understand
conflict situations.

As a woman coming from Delhi, I was largely considered an outsider
in Kashmir. However, my interviewees often remarked that due to some
resemblance with the Kashmiris, my identity could easily be mistaken.
That, however, didn't mean much, as I showed my ID and mentioned my
place of residence and religion in the interactions. Not that the people were
unwelcoming—in fact Kashmiris in the valley are by far the most hospitable
people I have come across—but a researcher coming from Delhi raised their
suspicion and people chose their words cautiously. My Kashmiri friend,
Abid, did a phenomenal job in clearing out their doubts and making them
feel comfortable with the purpose of my questions, and more important, with
my presence. His Kashmiri identity, his gender, along with the fact that he
was working for human rights in an international NGO helped in gaining the
trust of the people.

My gender identity also had a huge role to play in the field research. Men
were mostly not comfortable in talking about their experiences of humiliation
and shame in my presence. For instance, ex-militants, surrendered militants,
and other men who described their experiences of violence and physical "torture" preferred to share some stories and show their wounds in my absence.
On the other hand, male security personnel were proud to share their "brave
and courageous" stories in my presence, which of course is not surprising.
Women interviewees, especially mothers of militants killed, were not only
comfortable, but trusted me enough to share their grief and pain. My daughter's presence (then only aged around a year or two) in the initial field trips
also affected the response of women I interviewed. They were more open
to sharing their experience of loss as mothers. We sat together through long
silences to process their pain and my own emotions in response to their loss.
Being accompanied by a Kashmiri man was an advantage; however, there
were times when my friend was asked the reason for accompanying a woman.
It was not considered appropriate for an unmarried man to publicly walk with
an unrelated young woman, unless she was his teacher. I became more aware
of this problem when he was questioned at the office of a separatist leader in

Kashmir. I am very grateful that Abid didn't give up on me even after such stressful interrogation.

My very first interview was with an ex-militant in Budgam district. I was nervous to say the least, not only because of my anticipation of his reaction, but also because my impression of Kashmiri militants was shaped by mainstream Indian news channels, newspapers, and Bollywood movies that portrayed them as "ruthless" and as "fanatic" terrorists. This interview and the subsequent ones made me realize the huge role of media and popular culture in the construction and circulation of dominant narratives of "us" and "them." To my utmost surprise, the surrendered and ex-militants were not only welcoming but answered all questions patiently. Of course, there were a few interviewees who were not happy to meet me. I remember one instance in particular. An ex-militant, in an interview, asked me to cover my forehead and asked my local friend to recite a few verses of the Quran. He was not very pleased by the answer and eventually refused to give an interview. He went on to threaten to put an explosive in my pen. I could understand his anger and frustration, but I must confess, I was very scared to lose my own life, especially because my then two-year-old daughter along with my mother were waiting back at the hotel. On our way back, my interlocutor and I were stuck in a huge traffic jam due to the growing flood situation in Srinagar in September 2014. Those were moments of great introspection, questioning my own passion and the need for risking my life.

My identity of a researcher from the "outside" without any association to the network of recognized academics and activists in Kashmir or Delhi, seemed to also raise suspicion among NGOs who usually arrange meetings and interviews for research or journalistic purposes. This was clearly evident when a human rights organization denied me "permission" to conduct interviews in Kunan Poshpora villages. I understood their concern for the well-being of the rape victims, but at that time, I felt the survivors, or their families, could themselves have refused to give interviews. The male inhabitants of Kunan Poshpora didn't refuse for the interview to be conducted but asked me to go to the human rights organization to seek permission. "It is this organization that determines if you can conduct interview with the survivors or not"—a villager had said.[3] The strong hold of the civil society actors in determining who was worthy of conducting interviews raised all sorts of questions in my mind regarding knowledge production and construction of dominant human rights narratives. I had extensively referred to their material on human rights violations, and I went back to some other mentioned cases on the field to check their documentation. All the cases were accurately documented—that gave me a sense of relief and a chance to reflect upon my own vantage point as an outsider. In such reflections, I realized that more than my own ambition and need to produce authentic research, what was important is the emotional well-being of the survivors of violence. Instead of remind-ing them of the past trauma, it is indeed a better research practice to refer to their previous interviews and statements, if they had already given. So, I only looked up the existing interviews of rape survivors and made it a rule to first check existing sources in future research as well.

The self-reflexivity of the researcher is not only an important but also a crucial part of field research. Although, a large body of literature in anthro-pology, feminist, postcolonial, and decolonial studies include reflection of the field researcher, but it does not receive the attention and acknowledgement it deserves generally in the academy. Reflection on researcher's positionality is significant to understand the power relations between the researchers and the interviewees. As Henry, Higate, and Sanghera (2009) rightly argue that the political locatedness of the researcher needs to be continually reflected upon by the researchers, not as an exercise in navel-gazing, but as the basis of transformative politics. Quite often, due to the illusion of objectivity, the researcher assumes their position does not make much of a difference over the information gathered. However, the researcher's positionalities play a huge role in influencing the ways in which interviewees participate and the research is affected. Henry, Higate, and Sanghera (2009) suggest important questions to consider while conducting research: "Does it matter whether a researcher is white and female? Is she, he, or they academic? Who is the research for—UN, the University or an NGO?" The reflection on these questions definitely opens up spaces to "consider the boundaries interfaces of power relations and knowledge systems between the researcher and the researched."

My field research experience involved constant reflection of my political situatedness and multiple positionalities such as a female, Indian, outsider, non-Muslim, and the influence each had on the research. My positioning unconsciously also impacted the research questions and the way they are perceived and answered by the interviewees.

On the other hand, I also reflected upon what seemed to be a "fluidity" of boundaries between the researcher and the interviewee (Schulz, 2020). There was a profound impact of the stories and the pain of my interviewees on my own personal and emotional evolution. These conversations and exchanges played a significant role in making sense of my own life choices and paths. Even though I was not in touch with most of my interviewees after the field work, but their words stayed with me and even provided solace at times of my own personal loss and pain. It was a sort of an emotional osmosis that not just transformed the research process but also my own perceptions of the everyday lived experiences. There is one certain take away from my field work—an impossibility to conduct an "objective" and "distant observation" in a conflict affected society. Talking to the stakeholders requires reflective empathy and losing a sense of the rigid perception of oneself. Reflecting upon each interview is a spiritual process, one that involves a deep evaluation of the researcher's own perspective.

I try to let the field speak through the pages in this book. A big challenge, however, both during and while articulating the research, was navigating the exploitative nature of academic research. No matter how much I try to claim or believe that this research does not exploit the experiences of the locals; there is no denying that it is part of a larger academic endeavor that makes use of the lived realities of people to create and substantiate theories. My only hope is that the book will provide avenues to understand gender and conflict from a different perspective and readers find themselves connected to the voices and context of Kashmir. My vantage point, as a non-Kashmiri researcher of gender who often found herself wondering about the truth of the Kashmir conflict and resistance, will also hopefully be relatable to other non-Kashmiri Indians and interested people from other countries.

Organization of the Book

In this introduction, I have touched upon the gaps in the study of gender in conflicts, the meaning of agency as used in this book. I have also laid out the methodology and reflections on my own positionality as a researcher along with the ethical dilemmas and emotional challenges. I divide the remaining book into the following chapters.

Chapter 2

In this chapter, I contextualize the discussion by providing a brief historical background of the conflict and the Kashmiri resistance movement, for the readers to easily navigate through the various stages of the conflict. I also provide an outline of the growth of militancy and the subsequent changes that it underwent over a period of almost three decades. This will help the readers in situating the discussion around militarized masculinities both in the past and the present elaborated in chapters 3 and 4. In the latter half of the chapter, I make conceptual clarifications around the usage of the terms "hegemonic masculinity," "military/ militarized masculinities," and "Islamic and militant masculinities," along with the concept of conflict-related sexual violence (CRSV) against men and their agency, used in the context of demobilized militarized masculinities (in chapter 4). In doing so, I engage with the existing literature (especially in the last two decades) on the meanings attached to these different masculinities. Such a discussion will provide clarity and better understanding toward the employment of these terms in the Kashmiri context. As previously mentioned, the book foregrounds the idea of multiple masculinities, or a mosaic of masculinities, in the Kashmir conflict. However, due to the limitations of scope, I restrict the analysis to the military/militarized masculinities of both the state and non-state actors. This chapter will provide the suitable conceptual parameters to follow the interplay of militarized masculinities in Kashmir discussed in the following part of the book.

Chapter 3

This chapter explores one part of the competing military masculinities—represented by the Indian state armed forces. Here, I discuss the idealized military masculinity discussed in the existing feminist IR literature and how it is enacted and represented in Indian context. Furthermore, I explore the masculine ideals, values and practices associated with the Indian army in the Kashmir valley. In doing so, I attempt to move beyond the pre-dominant association of military masculinity with violence of men and explore the particular ways in which security personnel identify themselves as men and perceive manhood in their actual lived experiences. I use broad ethnographic research in order to uncover the meaning of masculinity and the attempts to hegemonize those meanings. I employ eclectic research tools and aids like interviews, slogans, graffiti, a study of the training methods and psychological warfare, representation in Bollywood movies, and so on. Each conflict setting has a different enactment of masculinities, and this chapter throws light on the nuances of the idealized military masculinity embedded in Kashmir, keeping in mind the political context of Hindu nationalism in mainland India. In the discussions, the chapter also highlights the notion of challenge or contestation as a significant part of masculine expectations. The subtle ways and indicators are highlighted through which the state forces challenge the manhood of the non-state actors and vice versa.

Chapter 4

Here, the attention is turned toward the second part of the competing militarized masculinity, represented by the nonstate actors who were militants or aspired to be a part of the "new" militancy. In this chapter, I explore the understanding and perception of manhood from a militancy perspective. I look at two different models of militancy—of the late 1980s and after 2010—that provided a platform for young men to reassert their manhood in the Kashmiri armed resistance. Interviews with former militants (both ex-militants and surrendered militants), along with those of the young boys who participated in the stone-pelting movement of 2008 and 2010, are an integral part of this chapter. Later, I also discuss the demobilized masculinities and how reintegrated former militants and male survivors of physical and (sometimes) sexual violence navigate the gender expectations and exercise their agency.

Chapter 5

In this chapter, I examine how the idea of women's agency engages with the militarized masculinities in the Kashmir. In doing so, I first discuss the significance of maternal symbolism used both in the Indian army camps and in the resistance movement. Imageries of *Bharat Mata* (Mother India) that are based on the Hindu conceptualization of femininity on the one hand, and, on the other, of the "kind," "grieving," and "sacrificing" mother in the Kashmiri resistance movement. These are important frames to not only confine femininity but also asserting the militarized masculinities. Furthermore, I highlight women's role in reinforcing militant masculinity through different resistance practices. As a way to understand the unique form of agency exercised by women in the resistance movement, I explore the role of two significant women leaders to understand their perception and engagement with patriarchy. In the latter half of the chapter, I look at the ways in which women deal with the challenges of absence and presence of their menfolk. Here, by discussing some narratives of the wives of former militants, widows of killed militants, and half-widows, I argue that along with the entanglement with masculinities, the victimization and agency of women also need to be studied as a simultaneous phenomenon instead of as binaries. Finally, I also look at the role of elected women representatives in *panchayat halqas* (self-governing bodies in the villages) to understand how they grapple with the patriarchal expectations of the state duties on the one hand and nonstate armed resistance groups on the other. Women's creative conformity and subversive nature of agency is explained in relational terms in this chapter. With a primary focus on empirical research, I build upon the existing attempts of feminist literature on nuancing women's agency in Kashmir and extend the understanding of agency by incorporating a masculinities perspective. The particular ways in which men reassert control and/or change their outlook on patriarchy/gender roles provide an important context to understand the expectations under which women perform their perceived roles in conflict. This chapter also provides an analysis of how masculinities and femininities are co-constructed by both men and women.

Chapter 6

This chapter concludes the book by pulling the discussed threads to, first, show the importance and relevance of studying masculinities in the Kashmir conflict. The study of the contestation of militarized masculinities aids in providing a context to the gender roles, behavior, and expectations in which both men and women co-construct and reproduce patterns of gender performativity. Second, I discuss the new and inclusive understanding of agency brought about in the book that entails ways in which both men and women navigate their lived realities and experiences in conflict. Also, how the idea of women's agency is further nuanced through an engagement with masculinities discourse. Third, I discuss the significance of employment of a combination of decolonial, feminist, and ethnographic research methods to arrive at a comprehensive understanding of gender dimensions in conflict through the context of the Kashmir.

REFERENCES

Ackerly, B. A, Friedman, E.J, Menon, K., & Zalewski, M. "Research Ethics and Epistemic Oppression." *International Feminist Journal of Politics*. Vol. 22, No. 3, 2020: 309–11.

Bhutalia, Urvashi. (ed). *Speaking Peace: Women's Voices from Kashmir*. New Delhi: Kali for Women, 2002.

Björkdahl, A., and Selimovic, J. M. "Gendering Agency in Transitional Justice." *Security Dialogue*. Vol. 46, No. 2, 2015: 165–82.

Bucar, Elizabeth M. *Creative Conformity: The Feminist Politics of US Catholic and Iranian Shi'I Women*. Washington: Georgetown University Press, 2011.

Butler, Judith. *Gender Trouble: Feminism and the Subversion of Identity*. New York: Routledge, Chapman and Hall, Inc. 1999.

Fujii, Lee Ann. "Shades of Truth and Lies: Interpreting Testimonies of War and Violence." *Journal of Peace Research*. Vol. 47, No. 2, 2010: 231–41.

Henry, M., Higate, P., and Sanghera, G. "Positionality and Power: The Politics of Peacekeeping Research." *International Peacekeeping*. Vol. 16, No. 4, 2009: 467–82.

Kazi, Seema. *Between Democracy and Nation: Gender and Militarization in Kashmir*. New Delhi: Women Unlimited, 2008.

Mahmood, Saba. "Feminist Theory, Embodiment and the Docile Agent: Some Reflections on the Egyptian Islamic Revival." *Cultural Anthropology*. Vol. 16, No. 2, 2001: 202–36.

Malik, Inshah. *Muslim Women, Agency, and Resistance Politics: The Case of Kashmir*. Switzerland: Palgrave Macmillan, 2019.

Manchanda, Rita. *Women, War, and Peace in South Asia: Beyond Victimhood to Agency*. New Delhi: Sage Publications, 2001.

McNay, L. *Gender and Agency. Reconfiguring the Subject in Feminist Social Theory*. Cambridge, UK: Polity Press, 2000.

Parashar, Swati. *Women and Militant Wars: Politics of Injury*. London and New York: Routledge, 2014.

Ray, Ayesha. "Kashmiri Women and the Politics of Identity." *SHUR Final Conference on Human Rights*. Rome: Luiss University, 2009.

Schulz, Philipp. "Recognizing Research Participants' Fluid Positionalities in (Post-) Conflict Zones." *Qualitative Research*. 2020: 1–18.

Shepherd, Laura J. "Sex, Security, and Superhero(in)es: From 1325 to 1820 and Beyond." *International Feminist Journal of Politics.* Vol. 13, No. 4, 2011: 504–21.

Sjoberg, L., and Gentry, C. *Mothers, Monsters, Whores: Women's Violence in Global Politics.* London/New York: Zed Books, 2007.

Touquet, Heleen, and Schulz, Philipp. "Navigating Vulnerabilities and Masculinities: How Gendered Contexts Shape the Agency of Male Sexual Violence Survivors." *Security Dialogue.* 2020. Available at: https://journals.sagepub.com/doi/full/10.1177/0967010620929176.

Wood, Elisabeth J. "The Ethical Challenges of Field Research in Conflict Zones." *Qualitative Sociology.* Vol. 29, 2006: 373–86.

NOTES

1. For example, see, R. W, Connell. *Masculinities.* Cambridge, UK: Polity Press, 1995; Brandon Hamber, "Masculinity and Transitional Justice: An Exploratory Essay," *The International Journal of Transitional Justice.* Vol. 1, Issue 3, 2007: 375–90; Henri Myrttinen, "Disarming Masculinities, Women, Peace and Security," Issue 4, 2003: 37–46; Chrisitine. Beasely, "Rethinking Hegemonic Masculinity in a Globalising World." *Men and Masculinities.* Vol. 11, Issue 1, 2008: 86–103; Claire Duncanson, "Hegemonic Macsulinity and the Possibility of Change in Gender Relations." *Men and Masculinities.* Vol. 18, Issue 2, 2015: 231–48; GuÐrún Sif FriÐriksdóttir, "Soldiering as an Obstacle to Manhood? Masculinities and Ex-Combatants in Burundi," *Critical Military Studies.* Vol. 7, Issue 1, 2018: 61–78; Elise Feron, *Wartime Sexual Violence Against Men: Masculinities and Power in Conflict Zones.* London: Rowman & Littlefield, 2018; Maria Eriksson Baaz and Maria Stern, *Sexual Violence as a Weapon of War? Perceptions, Prescriptions, Problems in the Congo and Beyond.* New York: Zed Books, 2013; David Duriesmith, *Masculinity and New War: The Gendered Dynamics of Contemporary Armed Conflict.* Routledge, 2019; Philipp Schulz, *Male Survivors of Wartime Sexual Violence: Perspectives from Northern Uganda.* Oakland: University of California Press, 2021.

2. A term that came up in one of the many discussions with Henri Myrttinen.

3. Personal Interview as on 30/08/2014.

Chapter 2

Providing a Roadmap

Historical Background and Conceptual Parameters

The self-perception and performance of gender identities in the Kashmir conflict cannot be understood in a single manner. It is a dynamic process and plays out differently in accordance with the changes in political conditions. Both men and women have made sense of their gender roles and expectations in relation to the changing contextual realities. The historical mapping of the Kashmiri resistance also suggests the varied nature of gender performativity, practices, and expectations. Also, this performativity entails a strong intersection with Muslim consciousness and identity in the valley. Women belonging to different classes—both elite and nonelite—have historically played a significant role in the Kashmiri resistance. However, how they perceive their position and identity as a Muslim woman, the practices they employ to claim their space in the political sphere, and the creative ways in which they exercise political agency have all have undergone multiple changes over a period of time. Similarly, how men understand the gender expectations, roles, and behavior has not remained static. Masculinity, as a concept, is dynamic, because the ideal way of being a man changes with transformed political realities. The dynamism attached to masculinities is quite visible in the Kashmir conflict, especially due to the changes in militancy and methods of resistance. The fluid nature of masculinity is, however, not only limited to the non-state actors; the particular ways of doing male have also undergone changes within the Indian army and other state armed forces.

Before exploring how the state and non-state actors perceive of and enact masculinities, this chapter provides a conceptual and historical map for the rest of the book. In the first half of the chapter, I provide a brief historical background of the Kashmir conflict and resistance. This is to equip the readers to navigate the changes in the perceived masculinities discussed in the subsequent chapters. In the latter half of the chapter, I explain the meanings associated with multiple masculinities especially with regard to terms like "militarized masculinity," "ideal/hegemonic masculinity," "Islamic and militant (*Mujahid*) masculinities," and "Conflict related sexual violence against men," borrowed from the existing critical masculinities studies and are used frequently in this book. The conceptual clarification is also important in order to explore the suitability and relevance of these concepts in the context of Kashmir.

THE KASHMIR CONFLICT: HISTORICAL BACKGROUND

The historical understanding of the Kashmir conflict and resistance is significant to make sense of the present lived experiences of the Kashmiri locals in the valley. It is, however, a challenging task to write an objective account of the Kashmiri past because historical narratives vary from one vantage point to another. The background I sketch here is based on my own understanding developed through oral histories, narratives, and secondary literature (written by both Kashmiri and non-Kashmiri authors). The conflict in Kashmir is usually traced back to the partition of the Indian subcontinent into two countries—India and Pakistan—in accordance with the Mountbatten plan in 1947. The princely states of the British India were given the choice to accede to either India or Pakistan, under the Indian Independence Act of July 18, 1947. Maharaja Hari Singh, the Dogra king, decided to accede to India despite the contestation and resistance from within Kashmir. The Dogra dynasty had ruled Kashmir since 1846, when their king, Gulab Singh Dogra, had signed the Treaty of Amritsar with the British East India Company. The treaty was a result of Gulab Singh's collaboration with the British in the First Anglo-Sikh war. Through this treaty, Gulab Singh acquired Kashmir with all its dependencies and in return paid 7.5 million Nanak Shahis, the currency of the Sikh empire, which ruled Kashmir before the Dogras took over (Whitehead, 2007).

Throughout its rule, the Dogra regime faced major resistance from the Kashmiris. Scholars and historians are divided about the causes for the Kashmiri resistance and protests against the Dogra rulers. The communal reasons behind such challenges—a Muslim majority being ruled by a Hindu family and the dislike towards anti-Muslim policies—seem to be a dominant narrative. However, writings of Kashmiri scholars and historians reveal that the struggle was "non-communal and directed against the administration of the state and was in no manner against non-Muslims" (Bazaz, 1954). Starting from protests against oppressive taxation policies for shawl weavers and the Rahdaari policy under Gulab Singh, and later more spontaneous, organized armed resistance of 1930s, especially after the formation of All Jammu and Kashmir Muslim Conference in 1931, presented a constant challenge for the Dogra rulers (Rai, 2004; Thorp, 2011). The Kashmiri pandits[1] also protested for their inclusion in the administrative jobs of the Dogra state. Muslim women, especially from the lower sections, actively participated in mass protests against the Dogra rule across Kashmir (Bazaz, 1954).

The All Jammu and Kashmir Muslim Conference was converted into the National Conference (at present, a dominant party in Kashmiri politics) in 1939 under the leadership of Sheikh Abdullah. In May 1946, Sheikh Abdullah launched the Quit Kashmir Movement against Maharaja Hari Singh. Muslim men and women enthusiastically joined the movement defying the discriminatory policies. In this context, scholars like Whitehead and Malik highlight the active role of Muslim women belonging to the lower classes such as Zoone Gojri in the movement (Whitehead, 2017; Malik, 2019). The women belonging to the elite Muslim class later joined in the movement to claim a space for themselves.

Sheikh Abdullah along with other National Conference leaders were soon jailed. Sheikh Abdullah's wife, Akbar Jehan, became actively involved in the anti-Dogra protests and raised money and collected donations for the persecuted Kashmiri people (Khan, 2014). The turbulence in Kashmiri politics further heightened when the tribal groups, supported by Pakistan, entered Kashmir in October 1946 to save their Muslim brethren and avenge the "mistreatment" of the Poonch Muslims by the Dogra rulers. They called it the "holy war" and took over the Western areas. Hundreds of Hindus and Sikhs were killed in the process. Alongside, an armed rebellion and anti-Muslim violence rose in Jammu. In the middle of the ongoing political troubles in Kashmir, the Maharaja sought military help and reluctantly agreed to formally accede to India (Akbar, 2002; Habibullah, 2008). The Indian troops came to defend Srinagar and National Conference's armed volunteers assisted them. Women's involvement and participation in the institutional defense mechanisms through the establishment of the Women's Defence Corps was quite striking. As Whitehead (2017) notes,

> The women's section of the militia, the Women's Self Defence Corps as it was known, was established when the threat to Srinagar was still acute. Stories circulated—perhaps exaggerated, but with a basis in fact—that the tribal forces had raped and abducted women, particularly, non-Muslims, as they advanced Eastwards along the Jhelum river. The idea behind the militia was that the women of Srinagar would be able to defend their honour should the city be overrun.

Although the Indian army had managed to successfully push back the tribals from Srinagar, a UN-mandated ceasefire resulted in the formation of the Pakistan administered Kashmir, also popularly known as "Azad Kashmir" by the local population. This region consists of the western and northwestern areas of the former princely state. During this period, women fighters continued receiving firearms and rifle training. However, by the end of 1948, the women's militia was disbanded and the men's militia was incorporated into the India's armed forces. Women's militia is, however, still remembered as a moment of empowerment for Kashmiri women. Indeed, rifle-carrying women appeared on two salient documents of the time: the cover of National Conference's 1944 manifesto, "New Kashmir," and on "Kashmir Defends Democracy," a propaganda pamphlet produced in 1948 in support of Sheikh Abdullah and the accession to India. These powerful images, as Whitehead (2017) asserts, projected "an emphatic demonstration that the era of princely rule was over."

An interim government was formed and Sheikh Abdullah became the prime minister (the position was called chief minister only from 1965) in 1948. At the United Nations (through the UN Security Council Resolution No. 47), India promised to conduct a plebiscite to confirm the accession.[2] The promise however was never fulfilled denying Kashmiris the right to self-determination and is, accordingly, regarded as one of the main reasons for the continued discontent of the Kashmiris with the Indian state. In 1949, the UN military observers arrived to supervise the ceasefire between India and Pakistan until the promised plebiscite was held. The Indian side of Kashmir was divided into two administrative territories—Jammu and Kashmir (J&K). The formation of the constituent assembly in 1950, resulted in Sheikh Abdullah resuming power. However, the Indian constitution made provision for Article 370, that granted considerable autonomy to the new state of J&K. It became operative in 1952, through the Delhi Agreement that was signed between Sheikh Abdullah and Indian government, which provided for the autonomy of the state within India and the autonomy for the regions within the state (Noorani, 2011).This was strongly protested by Hindu right-wing forces, especially Jan Sangh, which criticized Article 370 under *Ek Pradhan, Ek Vidhan, Ek Nishan* ("One PM, one constitution, one flag") slogan.

Meanwhile, Sheikh Abdullah and his supporters proactively demanded referendum (Gockhami, 2007). The continued reluctance of the Indian state made Abdullah critical of India in the long run and fostered Kashmiri nationalism, which was decidedly anti-India. Abdullah's use of state assembly as a platform for referendum politics started being viewed as a threat to the Indian state. As a result, Abdullah was arrested and removed from prime ministership in 1953. He and his aides were also accused of secretly conspiring against the Indian state, which came to be known as the "Kashmir conspiracy case."

Following the arrests, there were widespread protests by his followers and few people were killed by the police forces. Ghulam Mahmad Bakshi took over as the prime minister and Indian state control was strengthened during this period. The local people in Kashmir remember the Bakshi regime as corrupt and disconnected from people's aspirations for autonomy. The cause of the referendum was taken further through the initiation of the Plebiscite Front in 1955. During this time, several armed groups also emerged in Kashmir mainly due to the disillusionment and discontent that arose from the failed promise of the Indian state and the inability of National Conference to deliver the promise of freedom. They believed that a solution could only arrive through an armed struggle. The Mujahid Home Front was functioning since 1948 and later, Young Men's League and Al-Fatah also began operations against the Indian state (Farman Ali, 2012).

This period from 1950–1970 involved three simultaneous political activities in Kashmir: first, the emerging armed resistance inspired by the Algerian struggle against the French and the Palestinian struggle against Israel; second, a movement started by the Plebiscite Front to educate people on the importance of demanding referendum; and third, the Bakshi regime strengthening India's control on Kashmir and keeping tabs on the activities of Plebiscite front and curbing other forms of dissent. By the time Abdullah was released in 1964, his support had declined due to the failure of the plebiscite movement. During this time, there was a public shift toward Islamic identity and discussions around strengthening resistance against the growing authoritarian state. Interviewed locals in the valley recall that they were disillusioned by the politics of National Conference, especially after Abdullah signed the Indira-Sheikh accord in 1975, which allowed him to become the chief minister of J&K state. There were widespread protests by people against Abdullah signing the accord. Women actively participated by raising slogans of "Rai Shomeri arakh Dobas, Aalve Babas Mobarakah" (The demand for plebiscite is annulled, congratulations to our worthless leader) (Malik, 2019). The destiny of Kashmiris in the valley seemed to be caught in between the promises, their leaders, and a larger game of power. People remember this accord as a betrayal by the National Conference and believe that it changed the history of J&K state by giving maximum powers to the center. Sajad Gani Lone, the Peoples' Conference chairman articulates this sentiment: "When they (National Conference) are out of power they remember all erosions made to Article 370 but when they are in power, they kill with impunity." He further adds, "The people of J&K deserve to know what happened, given that the ones (National Conference leaders) who destroyed the special status through the Indira [Gandhi]-Sheikh accord are now sermonizing people about human rights violations and killings" (KL News Network, 2019).

By the early 1980s, there were visible attempts at refashioning and reclaiming of Islamic teachings into a powerful weapon for the resistance movement. Muslim revivalist thoughts and literature was made available to the youth through the classrooms and religious sermons. Jamat-e-Islami (Congregation of Islam) started the reformation of Islam. The Jamat followed the ideology of reintroduction of the Sharia law and regarded it as the source for achieving political freedom. The efforts of Jamat-e-Islami contributed towards asserting a Muslim identity of Kashmir. The ideas propagated by the Jamat mobilized and ignited enthusiasm among the youth, particularly the students. The widespread discontent with the party politics of National Conference and the death of Sheikh Abdullah in 1982, led to a political shift in the Kashmiri politics. Islamic Students League (ISL), which also had a women's wing, organized student mobilization around the Muslim revivalist ideas. In addition to ISL, an all-women outfit, *Dukhtaran-e-Millat* (the daughters of the nation), began as a project in 1982 to educate women about their rights and duties in Islam. In July 1984, Indira Gandhi dismissed Farooq Abdullah, Sheikh Abdullah's son and political successor, and replaced him with G. M. Shah, a disaffected member of the National Conference. Farooq Abdullah's abrupt dismissal "deeply offended a new generation of politically conscious Kashmiris" (Ganguly, 1996). Also, the increasing reaffirmation of the Muslim identity for political liberation and political events such as the hanging of Maqbool Bhat in Tihar Jail in Delhi 1984 were a trigger to the start of armed resistance in Kashmir. The next two years were marked by strikes, demonstrations, and bombings and created a politically disturbed state of affairs. The chief minister, G.M. Shah was unable to curb the rising tide of violence, and was soon dismissed. Indira Gandhi's son, Rajiv Gandhi, who became the prime minister after his mother's assassination, signed an accord with Farooq Abdullah in November 1986, making him chief minister of Kashmir. This was not taken well by the new generation of the Kashmiri youth. As Ganguly (1996) mentions, "Whatever sympathy and legitimacy that Farooq had in the eyes of the emergent Kashmiri youth was now lost. The accord reduced him to the stature of a mere stalking horse for the Congress."

A political coalition called Muslim United Front (MUF) was formed in 1987, led by Jamat-e-Islami in order to contest elections against the alliance between National Conference and the Congress party. There was a high turnout of voters supporting the MUF, however the polls were rigged. Voters were intimidated, ballot boxes were tampered with, and candidates of MUF threatened. The rigged election convinced the younger generation that government at the center would not consider their political rights, and in the absence of any institutional recourse, armed rebellion and violence became an important way to express their discontent. Several key insurgent leaders such as Yasin Malik, Shabir Shah, and Javed Mir were earlier polling agents of the MUF.

Afghanistan's successful resistance to Soviet invasion in 1989, the Palestinian intifada and resurgence of transnational Islam in the wake of Iranian revolution—all reinforced the enthusiasm among young Kashmiri men, who crossed over the Line of Control (LOC) into the Pakistan-administered Kashmir in large numbers to receive arms training. The insurgency reached its peak in early 1990s, resulting in the loss of several thousand lives and forced a large number of Kashmiri Hindus (pandits) from their homes.

The most prominent of the insurgent groups was the Jammu and Kashmir Liberation Front (JKLF). Started by former ISL members, it strived to fight for the freedom of Kashmir and form an independent nation inspired by teachings of Islam. For the longest time, JKLF was the indigenous underground movement of young people, which Behera (2006) calls the first phase of Kashmiri insurgency. Led within the valley by the "Haji" group, the JKLF had widespread support among the Muslim Kashmiris in the valley, especially the youth. Likewise, the political units that had formed the MUF, created their respective militant wings.[3] Another key actor was the militant wing of Jamat-e-Islami, Hizbul Mujahideen, which was based in Sopore. Its objective was reunification with Pakistan. There were some other small groups that favored Pakistan such as Hizbullah, Al-Umar Mujahideen, Lashkar-i-Toiba, Ikhwan-ul-Mujahideen Hiz-bul Momineen, and Tehriq-ul-Mujahideen.

Young men between the age of sixteen and thirty from several districts of Kashmir, joined different militant groups and crossed the LOC to receive arms training. In 1989, militants of the JKLF kidnapped Dr. Rubaiya Sayeed, the daughter of the home minister Mufti Muhammed Sayeed. They demanded the release of five militants, including JKLF leader Sheikh Hamid and the brother of Maqbool Bhat in return for Rubaiya's freedom. The militants were released and Rubaiya was also freed, unharmed. There was a triumphant procession in Srinagar on the release of the militants. This showed huge support for the indigenous militancy movement. The incompetency of the Indian government to address the political instability led to an atmosphere of political disorder. There was an increase in the frequency of bombings and demonstrations. People belonging to varied professions such as teachers, lawyers, and doctors all came on the streets. Women played an important role as resisters during this phase. "The fight was not just between the militants and the security forces, but now assumed the form of total insurgency of the entire population" (Puri, 1993). There were slogans every day, loudspeakers on the mosques also encouraged people to come out. The overwhelming sentiment of Azadi (freedom and creation of an independent state) was highly visible during this early phase of militancy. The central government through the appointment of Jagmohan as the governor attempted to suppress resistance but failed.

Women's organizations proactively worked to support the cause of free-dom. Muslim Khawateen Markaz (MKM), an all-women's profreedom organization came into existence in 1987. Ordinary Kashmiri Muslim women supported the movement from their houses. They provided shelter, food and aid to the militants, smuggled weapons, and cleared areas of civilians ahead of attacks. They decorated their sons as bridegrooms to bring home Azadi (freedom) as their wives. Young women's enthusiasm to reproduce militants both literally and symbolically was visible in the popular slogan, *Pakistan Jaayenge, Do Roti Khaayenge, pet mein mujahid leke ayenge* ("We will go to Pakistan, eat two breads, and come back pregnant with a militant child") (Parashar, 2011). Mothers sang songs of glory, pride, and martyrdom in funer-als of their dead militant sons. The insurgency of late 1980s and early 1990s was not limited to the militant groups but included full support of the ordinary local people in the valley. Women's support provided the desired sanctity and validation to the movement.

The widespread support to the militancy, however, started shrinking in the late 1990s into early 2000s. Over a period of time, the militant groups were turning the guns on each other, and the masses began to get disillusioned with an increasingly fragmented militancy. Militancy had gradually become a lucrative profession. The support and respect that militancy had gained in the initial phase declined and what followed was a reign of terror and dik-tats from the militant groups, especially those involving foreign militants (Baweja, 1992). Women became more aware of the social crises that emerged such as deaths, enforced disappearances, sexual violence, and other grave human rights violations. Women's organisations such as MKM and other human rights organizations got involved in the social repair and the process for justice. Lack of platforms for grievance added more layers of discontent. Parveena Ahangar, whose eighteen-year-old son, Javed, went missing after he was picked up by the Indian Army in 1994, organized an Association of Parents of Disappeared Persons (APDP). With the increase in the disappear-ance cases, this organization has become the face of Kashmir's grief. On the tenth day of each month, mothers gather in a public park to grieve and remember their loved ones.

Later, the year 2008 marked the renewal of Kashmir's resistance move-ment, when the Indian government reached an agreement with the state of Jammu and Kashmir to transfer ninety-nine acres of forest land to the Amarnath Shrine Board (that facilitates the religious pilgrimage from main-land India to the Amarnath cave). People in Kashmir rendered this decision as a massive violation of Article 35 A and 370 that granted autonomy to the state. A large number of people gathered for a rally and protested against this decision (*New York Times*, 2008). Slogans like "Go Back India Go Back" and stones were pelted by young teenagers on the army vehicles. Indian armed forces indiscriminately fired from pellet guns to suppress the resistance.

In 2010, the killing of a young boy, Tufail Mattoo (caught in a clash between the stone pelters and police) ignited people's anger and gave rise to a fierce rebellion in the valley. Young girls came on the streets to confront and pelt stones at the Indian Army. Several young boys suffered pellet injuries, and many decided to join militancy. Kashmir once again saw a new form of indigenous militancy comprising of young, educated boys who posted pictures on social media platforms such as Facebook and became popular heroes in the valley. Women approved of and provided wholehearted support to the aspiring militants. In 2016, the leader of the new militancy, Burhan Wani, was killed by the Indian armed forces, which led to huge protests. Men and women gathered in large numbers at his funeral procession. Women sang songs of glory, praise, and freedom. The Indian state adopted repressive and violent methods to quell the growing dissent.

In August 2019, the Kashmiri politics took another turn. The right-wing Indian government abrogated Article 370 that granted special status to J&K state. A curfew was imposed, Kashmiri political leaders were house arrested and internet services were cut off for months after the decision was announced. The integrationists, represented by the Hindu right wing, were always opposed to the idea of granting a special status to a state within India. The eventual revocation of Article 370 was thus a celebratory moment for BJP (the ruling party) and its supporters, who believed it to be a step to "restore" Kashmiri history. They regarded it as a corrective to a grave mistake made by Jawaharlal Nehru and other Indian National Congress members, because the grant of special status was based on both a political and cultural misrepresentation of the valley as unique and isolated. In this context, Shonaleeka Kaul (2018), in her recent book, discusses *Rajatarangini*, an epic Sanskrit poem of nearly 8,000 verses, written by a Kashmiri called Kalhana in the twelfth century. Through the invocation of Rajatarangini that narrates the stories of Kashmir royal dynasties over more than a millennium, Kaul argues that "Kashmir was never isolated, but incredibly open and cosmopolitan, and overwhelming Indic in her genesis and composition rather than unique." The connected histories and entanglement between Kashmir and Indic subcontinent, according to her, shaped Kashmir's making. She further argues that the imposition of Article 370, created an artificial separation and its revocation has restored Kashmiri identity "in all its openness, pluralism and cosmopolitanism." Kaul's arguments reflect the views held by most Kashmiri Pandits that I have known and interviewed.

However, the attempts to demarcate a specific Indic identity to Kashmir, embodied in work of Kaul and other scholars have been extensively

criticized. Contemporary historians, such as, Luther Obrock (2020), are critical of Kaul's ambition of "recovering Kashmir as an ideological unit through
Sanskrit poetry." He further adds that unlike Kaul's claim, *Rajatarangini*
seems less an "assertion of identity or homeland and more a daring and auda-
cious experiment in self-assertion," and the text should instead be read as
trace of lives of real people expressed through Sanskrit. Similarly, Malavika
Kasturi and Mekhola Gomes (2020) also problematize the idea of nation tied
to the "Sanskritic culture" in Kaul's writings. The decontextualizing of texts
and reading them in a linear fashion, to fit into a preordained idea of India is
a concerning issue, as these scholars have expressed with regard to the ongoing practice of enabling majoritarian nationalism. To sum, various scholars
and political leaders have justified their position on Article 370 through the
use of selected historical narratives. Despite all claims of connected early
histories between Kashmir and India, one cannot overlook the political con-
tingencies and perhaps the miscalculations in the colonial/postcolonial past
that made it necessary to grant autonomous status to the state. It is important
to state here that the situation in Kashmir after the removal of Article 370 has
not improved in the manner promised by the government. The subsequent
lockdown of the valley after the revocation, arrest of political leaders, and
disruption of internet connectivity of the valley—all measures point toward
the continued discontent of the people.

MASCULINITIES: USAGE AND
CONCEPTUAL CLARIFICATIONS

The understanding of power relations in conflict societies is crucially
informed by gendered analyses. In this regard, both feminists and critical
masculinity scholars have highlighted the integral role of masculinity in conflicts and political violence. The pervasiveness of masculinity, however, is
naturalized to such an extent that it seems invisible. Michael Kimmel (1997)
accurately articulates this invisibility—"Masculinity is almost invariably
invisible in shaping social relations its ever-present specificity and significance shrouded in its constitution as the universal, the axiomatic, the neutral."
He further notes, "Masculinity assumes the banality of the unstated norm—
not requiring comment, let alone explanation" (Gardiner 2005; Kimmel,
1997). Keeping in view the privilege derived through this invisibility, this
book, through the case of Kashmir, attempts to make visible the mundane yet
norm-making masculine practices and behaviors in conflict, in order to highlight the existing power relations and their continued reproduction. However,
as described in the first chapter, masculinity is not monolithic, and this book
foregrounds the multiplicity of masculinities in its discussion on the Kashmir

conflict. Through a multiple-masculinities standpoint, this book further aims to arrive at a more nuanced assessment of power relations and diversity of gender hierarchies in conflict affected societies. In order to achieve this objective, it becomes imperative to first provide a few clarifications around varying concepts of masculinities and terminologies used in this book. The readers who are new to critical masculinities' literature, but interested in the context, may find the following sections conceptually loaded, so in chapter 6, I combine the theoretical discussion with the empirical analysis to show how and why studying masculinities matters through case of Kashmir. For the readers already familiar with the critical scholarship on men and masculinities (CSMM), but not so much with the context, the following sections maybe useful in highlighting the relevance or nonrelevance of the ongoing debates on masculinities in the context of Kashmir.

Ideal/Hegemonic Masculinity: Conceptual Debates and Relevance in Kashmir

In most simple terms, *masculinity* is defined as the widespread social norms and expectations to what it means to be a man. However, there is no singular, monolithic way or practice of masculinity. Scholars like Judith Large (2002) and others have already pointed out the existence of multiple ways of "doing male." These are shaped through different cultural, social, political, and economic contexts. Within these multiple versions of manhood, there is a dominant or an ideal form of masculinity—commonly known as the hegemonic masculinity—a concept initially propounded by Raewyn Connell. Hegemonic masculinity refers to a type of manhood that only a few men can actually achieve, while others position themselves in relation to it. Furthermore, Connell (1995) suggests that the idealized masculinity dominates over other masculinities, which are seen as subordinate to it. Also, hegemonic masculinity is culturally idealized, that is, it incorporates the behavior, attitudes, and practices that are seen as good and right for a man to have. Further, the characteristics and practices outlined of a typical man are also positively sanctioned as appropriate. Connell also shows that the hegemonic masculinity is the most powerful, culturally endorsed type of masculinity, which has subordinated other forms of masculinity as well as women and succeeded in positioning itself as superior. However, according to her, being hegemonic means that the dominance has to be achieved and constantly struggled for in face of the challenges from femininities and sub-ordinate masculinities. In that sense, producing consent from subordinated men is a key quality of hegemonic masculinity. The idea of hegemony in this context requires producing a situation whereby subordinated men not only position themselves to the idealized masculinity, but also see it as acceptable and sometimes the only possible way to live.

Over a period of time, the concept of hegemonic masculinity has become a subject of debate. Scholarship on critical masculinities in the past two decades has extensively engaged with hegemonic masculinity by both questioning and revisiting the idea. Demetriou (2001) and Moller (2007), for instance, criticize Connell's classification for its simplicity and inadequacy to understand masculinities in all their complexity. In this context, Beasley (2008) provides a significant case for revisiting hegemonic masculinity by narrowing the characterization of hegemonic masculinity as a political mechanism and differentiating this meaning from a usage dealing with authority of socially dominant men. She explains, "To put Connell's conception of hegemonic masculinity as a political mechanism, it is important to be able to disentangle hegemonic as legitimating from merely dominant types/ dominant actual men and their associated personality traits." Similarly, Flood (2002) points out that actual men may or may not conform to cultural ideals concerning masculinity, even when these are associated with power. Such contradictions and complexities are important to acknowledge and are overlooked in Connell's framework. Theo Hollander (2014), through his study of a small town in eastern Democratic Republic of Congo, also questions Connell's classification of hegemonic masculinity and subordinate masculinities in situations of extreme distress. He contends that Connell's model fails to capture the social inequalities and renegotiation of the masculine ideal. The idea that renegotiation is a dynamic, nonlinear, and sometimes a contradictory process that results in a new masculine subjectivity, defies the model of hegemonic masculinity. In a similar light, Sofia Aboim (2010) argues, "Any masculinity, as any man, as any individual is plural both in relation to the material positions that locate him in the social world and the cultural references that constitute his universe of meaning and significance." Beasley (2008) recommends employing language of "supra" and "sub" hegemonic masculinities to attend to the plurality and nuances of the term.

In studying masculinities in the Kashmir conflict, I borrow two important recommendations from Beasley's rethinking of hegemonic masculinity— the characterization of hegemonic masculinity as a political mechanism/ legitimating strategy (not only the personality traits of dominant men) and an emphasis on the culturally specific, postcolonial analyses of masculinities. I do not explore the supra- and sub-categories, however; I contend that hegemonic masculinity can be both plural and fluid, where hegemonic masculinities may even coexist and also change through adoption of new practices and styles of soldiering. Embedded in a culturally specific "postcolonial" context of Kashmir, this study shows the ways in which different actors (both state and non-state) aspire and compete to hegemonize their perceived masculinity as the ideal type, in order to legitimize their dominance in the conflict. In exploring the masculinities of the Indian army and the militancy in the Kashmir conflict, I believe that hegemonic masculinity is a useful concept to make sense of the contestation between the two militarized camps. Also, the changes and shifts in the military and militant masculinities and their power dynamics can be better understood through the lens of hegemonic masculinity. In this context, Duncanson's (2015) argument about the usefulness of hegemonic masculinities in militaries scholarship is relevant: "hegemonic masculinity has been a useful concept for explaining the dominance of men and masculinist foreign policies in a context of multiple, shifting and contradictory masculinities." However, Duncanson's optimism of dismantling hegemonic masculinity and the possibility of progressive social change of military masculinities (primarily focused on the global north) is still hard to decipher in the context of this study. I am not sure if softer changes in the attitude and practices of military men can be viewed as bringing progressive social change in the context of Kashmir. Having said that, I do agree that an empathetic approach to understanding men's relation to violence facilitates a more inclusive assessment of masculinities. To study men's association with violence, I also adopt Duncanson's approach to understand the construction of men's identities in a conflict with care rather than radically othering these.

Working through the empirical material on masculinities of Indian army personnel and ex-militants/surrendered militants and aspiring militants in chapters 3 and 4, I study three things broadly. First, I study the existence of multiple overlapping masculinities within the two militarized groups; second, the meaning attached to hegemonic masculinity (both in terms of personality traits and practices) in the Kashmir conflict in relation to the masculine contestations between the Indian Army and the militancy movement; third, the practices and ways which indicate the use of masculinity as a significant political mechanism to hegemonize the respective positions of both these actors. The masculinities in Kashmir entail interesting intersections and overlaps between hegemonic, military/militarized, and Islamic masculinities. In the following sections of this chapter, I explain the usage of the terms "military/militarized" and "Islamic" masculinities as used in this book.

Military/Militarized Masculinities

The study of military/militarized masculinities in the Kashmir conflict is a complex endeavor. On the one hand, in a heavily militarized conflict setting, military/militarized masculinities are not only pervasive, but also very direct (at least for a gender studies researcher)—as Morgan (1994) rightly explains "of all the sites where masculinities are constructed, reproduced and deployed those associated with war and military are some of the most direct." On the other hand, there are multiple intersections and simultaneous enactment of other masculinities and identities that make militarized masculinities research highly complex. Also, enactment of militarized masculinities not only include the traits and behavior of the men in combat/militaries (both state and non-state) but also the practices and ways of sustaining these masculinities. This book (in the third and fourth chapters) explores the masculinized traits, behavior, styles, and practices of militarized men both in the Indian state armed forces and those who were or aspire to be in the militancy movement. To examine the contestation and power relations among the militarized masculinities, I adopt a practice-oriented approach close to Theidon's (2009, 5) analysis of militarized masculinities in Colombia:

> [The practice approach] captures how individuals practice an embodied politics of masculinity that draws upon a diverse cultural repertoire of masculine behavior, which in turn is informed by one's class, ethnic, racial, religious and other identities.

My research of the military and militarized masculinities in Kashmir is driven by a curiosity to understand how violent forms of masculinities are forged and sustained. Due to an absence of a detailed exploration of such masculinities in the context of Kashmir, I draw from Theidon's, and perhaps other critical masculinities studies scholars' works from around the world that entail "the fusion of certain practices and images of maleness, with the use of weapons, the exercise of violence and performance of aggressive and violence forms of masculinities" (Theidon 2009, 5).

There is, however, always a danger involved in the study of military masculinities in conflict-affected regions, which is to equate masculinities in conflict with violence of men. The purpose of invoking military and militarized masculinities in this book is not to highlight how men and violence are inseparable categories in conflicts. Instead, I use these concepts to make more nuanced sense of manhood on the one hand, and show their overlaps and intersections with other forms of masculinity on the other. Feminist IR scholarship on conflicts (also in South Asia) has used the term "military masculinity" in a monolithic manner to denote the overwhelming association of violence with men. Myrttinen, Khattab, and Naujoks (2016), and feminists like Zalewski (2017) have pointed out the problems with the one-dimensional use of the term. This trend of oversimplifying military masculinity as violence of men has not helped much in addressing the gendered power relations or militarized violence; and instead has reinforced the gender binaries more. Through this study, I also hope to challenge this practice and show the fluid/intersectional nature of and within military/militarized masculinities in conflict.

Despite being conscious of warnings by scholars like Duriesmith and Ismail (2019), the broad framework used to study the contesting masculinities is methodological nationalism. This is because the nationalist narrative is intrinsically present in the challenges and practices of manhood in both the perspectives of state military personnel and ex/surrendered/aspiring militants. At the same time, I am, however, aware of the complexities and paradoxes involved in the performance of violent masculinities. Through the exploration of militarized masculinities of ex-militants and aspiring militants, I throw light on the existing diversity of masculinities and gender hierarchies among these men. Men representing the military or militarized masculinities may also simultaneously represent softer and marginalized masculinities or may even use agency to "unmake militarized masculinity" (Bulmer & Eichler, 2017) in the conflict. As Duriesmith and Ismail (2019, 156) aptly put it, "Adopting politics of scale will provide those studying militarized masculinities a new tool for uncovering the complex overlapping relationships of power that structure military practice."

These scales of masculinities are acknowledged in the successive chapters of the book. Along with the reflexivity around the multiplicity, overlaps, and intersections in gender hierarchies, I also pay particular attention to the ways in which agency is exercised by men who simultaneously represent both militarized and marginalized masculinities. Some examples used are the agency of demobilized militants who are ostracized and alienated, and of the (very few cases of) male survivors of physical and sexual violence. In studying the military masculinities, I also study the shifts that have taken place over a period of time. These shifts entail the change in perceived masculine traits, styles along with the practices and strategies adopted both by the Indian army and the militancy. The logic for analyzing the shifts is not to suggest the "progressive" or "positive" hegemonic masculinity of militarized men, but rather to simply acknowledge the constant need to negotiate and renegotiate masculine behavior and practices in conflict situations.

Finally, I also explore the intersection of the military and militarized masculinities with the religious identities of soldiers and ex-militants, respectively. Here, both Hindu nationalism and Islamic interpretations play an integral role in shaping masculine identities of the actors representing the respective camps. Given the complexities around uncovering the military/militarized masculinities in Kashmir, the epistemology cannot be restricted to a single method. The book borrows frames and methods prescribed by different scholars depending on their suitability in the context of Kashmir, such as politics of scale, practices, images, and an intersectional approach, while also entailing methodological nationalism.

Islamic and Mujahid (Militant) Masculinities

Religion plays an integral role in shaping gender identities in the present Kashmiri society. Based on the narratives of the interviewed ex-militants, boys who participated in the stone pelting movement, and mothers who lost their sons, one finds religion as a core motivation in the resistance movement. Especially in the study of the masculinity of ex-militants and aspiring militants and their different perceived ways of being a man, religious narratives seem to be significant. To study the intersections between militant masculinity and religion, I use concepts like "political Islam" and "Islamic masculinity" in the book, borrowed and understood through Duriesmith's (2018) illustrious work on the new war masculinities of Indonesian foreign fighters. The relevance and suitability of these terms, however, needs to be explained in the context of Kashmir. While doing so, this book also recognizes the problem of using Islamism as a generalizable term to study the Kashmiri society and resistance. This is for two reasons. First, Kashmiri resistance is historically built upon different versions of political consciousness and religious thought is only one of them. For instance, the early phase of Kashmiri nationalism led by Sheikh Abdullah was based on more secular foundations as compared to the late resistance that entailed more political Islamic elements. Second, even within the religious resistance politics, there are multiple scales of Islamic liberation ideals that have been perceived and implemented. For instance, on the one hand, there are more radical versions propagated by separatist organizations such as the Hurriyat party and Dukhtaran-e-Millat, but on the other hand, there is a hybrid version of Islamic influences and principles of secularism and coexistence with non-Muslim religions, represented by the Islamic Students League of 1980s and also by women organizations like Muslim Khawateen Markaz (MKM).

Keeping the multiplicity of Islamic liberation perspectives in mind, this book mainly grounds its analysis of political Islam and Islamic masculinities in the Kashmiri religious resistance from 1980s onward—a period when radical efforts at reinforcing the Muslim identity and consciousness started intensifying. During this time, the refashioning of traditional Islamic teachings to serve the purposes of the resistance movement resulted in extensive politicization of Islam. There were attempts to reintroduce the Shariah law as a source of political liberation (Malik, 2019). The Muslim revivalist thought circulated through sermons and radio programs, religious classes held by Jamat-e-Islami and darsgahs (centers imparting religious education to children and women), and religious education of women through Dukhatran-e-Millat, all facilitated the influence of religion on the public awareness. The following remark of a woman separatist leader (which will come again later in the book) highlights to some extent the significance of religion in

Kashmiri resistance and politics: "Islam is a way of life. It provides guidance to Muslims on how to live. Islam is also a guiding force for politics."[4]

The reassertion of the Islamic political ideology, not just in Kashmir but in other parts of the world sought to "modernize and militarize Islam to fight colonialism and more recently militarism" (Malik, 2019, 64). The Islamic reassertion in the Kashmiri resistance politics culminated into a violent resistance movement against the Indian state in 1989. As discussed earlier, former ISL leaders started the Jammu and Kashmir Liberation Front (JKLF), an organization with a goal to fight the Indian state and form an independent Islam inspired Kashmiri nation. During this period, when a number of young boys crossed the line of control to receive arms training in Pakistani administered Kashmir—a model of Islamic masculinity in Kashmir was widely accepted. This model drew heavily on the revivalist and militarized Islamic political project that defined the role of the Mujahid (warrior-fighter) as defender of the Muslim community in Kashmir. The retellings of the violent resistance phase of 1989 draw extensively on the narrative of the heroic resistance to external Muslim oppression. However, this model of militant masculinity is also shaped by non-Islamic sources such as Kashmiri folk traditions and revolutionary examples from non-Islamic histories. These are discussed in chapter 4.

The book keeps this model of Islamic manhood as a reference point to first understand how resistance practices and training methods contributed to shaping this as an idealized form of militant masculinity. Along with studying practices, it also extensively relies on the interviews of ex-militants and surrendered militants to study their perceived understanding of manhood. Second, the book also shows how this model of Islamic masculinity underwent a series of changes and transformations until 2016. Here, the new militancy that gained momentum under the leadership of Burhan Wani is relevant. The shaping up of the masculinity of the new militant heroes in relation to religion is explored also. Narratives of young boys aspiring to join the indigenous militancy movement in 2014 and 2015 are analyzed to understand the newer forms of perceived manhood, styles and practices to achieve the same.

Conflict Related Sexual Violence Against Men and Agency of Survivors

In chapter 4, I discuss conflict related sexual violence (CRSV) and gender-based violence (GBV) against men in the context of conversations around the demobilized militarized masculinities. Although few human rights reports in Kashmir suggest cases of sexual violence against civilian men, however, as previously mentioned, I limit my scope to studying masculinities of militarized men (along with their various intersections) in this book. In the conducted interviews, former militants shared their experiences of physical (and sexual) violence. They termed such experiences as "torture" and some-times "extreme torture." Some showed marks of their injuries of physical "torture" and also highlighted the techniques used by the Indian army. While physical violence is frequently discussed, sexual violence against men is not talked about in the Kashmir conflict. The conservative nature of Kashmiri society, along with very few avenues of support is perhaps responsible for the silence around sexual violence. As a result, there is limited theoretical and empirical exploration for the same. Responses of a few former militants in this research confirmed the existence of sexual violence although they adopted discretion in sharing the details and it is difficult to validate the data. Some reports of human rights violations compiled by prominent human rights organizations include few documented cases of sexual violence against men in detail. Overall, it is a challenging task to conceptualize CRSV against men in Kashmir due to the inadequate data. In the following part of this section, I explore the existing discussions around sexual violence against men in dif-ferent contexts around the world, to ground the contextual uniqueness of my own research findings discussed later in the book.

From a global perspective, different explanations are available for the occurrence of sexual violence in different conflict contexts. As Eriksson Baaz and Stern (2013) argue, these can be classified in two broad analytical categories: sexed (opportunistic) and gendered (strategic). The sexed analysis entails explanations that attribute male perpetrator's unfulfilled sexual desire and the "need" for a sexual release in stressful conditions. The gender lens throws light on the power relations as significant underlying factors in acts of sexual violence against men. In the gender analysis, sexual violence against men and women acts as an effective instrument for intimidation and humili-ation. More recent work proposes a combination of both these categories to explain and analyze conflict-related sexual violence (CRSV). CRSV against men and against women, is often an expression of dominance and power over the enemy. However, in CRSV, particularly against men, there is often a tendency to equate the survivor to a woman or a nonmasculine person. Scholars like Touquet and Gorris (2016) and Schulz (2020) have criticized such tendencies manifested in the usage of terminologies like "feminization," "emasculation," and "homosexualization" of the victim. Such usages over-shadow and invisibilize the agency of the survivors in rebuilding themselves and regaining their perceived sense of self.

Although a number of studies have emerged on CRSV against men, how-ever, this phenomenon still tends to be viewed as an exception to the norm. Also, CRSV against men is pre-dominantly analyzed in two extreme bina-ries in relation to masculinities—either as violence of male perpetrators or vulnerabilities of male victims (Schulz, 2020). I found that the most widely available reading material (during the period of my field research) on sexual violence against men (mainly on the internet) included false portrayals of sexual violence against men as "exceptions" that left men feeling "the most vulnerable." This leads to the reproduction of a problematic essentialist narrative. Parallel to the ways in which women's violence is constructed as an exception through narratives of "mother, "monster," and "whore" (Sjoberg and Gentry, 2007), men's victimhood is also constructed as an exception. Both the discourses are significant in upholding the gendered war narratives of "men as perpetrators" and "women as victims."

It is also important to point out the significance of framing of the term "torture" in documentation around sexual violence. Scholars like Michele Leiby (2009) have shown through their research that coding of sexual torture or abuses simply as torture can misrepresent the nature and patterns of sexual violence. As Leiby (2009) rightly argues, "Understanding how victims and reporting agencies conceptualize sexual violence is crucial to understand exactly what is captured in reported statistics on sexual violence and its use in war." Furthermore, the coding of CRSV against men simply as torture, makes sexual violence against men become an exception, an extreme instance, and that is problematic because it not only essentializes the experiences, but it also prohibit men from accessing harm responsive and sex health services (Sivakumaran, 2007; Schulz, 2020). The ways in which torture is codified varies from one context to another. Gray and Stern (2019) argue that torture is a slippery term, employable in multiple ways and filled with meanings that are neither fixed nor stable. In a similar way, the usage of "torture" differs in Kashmir and entails not only the sexual violence but all forms of physical violence during the arrest and detention. "Torture" is used commonly by the locals to highlight the extreme violence inflicted by the state armed forces on the Kashmiri Muslim men and women, both civilians and militants. The survivors of different forms of violence use "torture" to narrate their victimhood. In some ways, naming their experience torture provides them with the courage to voice out their difficult past experiences.

Male vulnerabilities and victimhood in conflict are often characterized as the loss of manhood due to the experiences of humiliation, shame, and intimidation. For a man, being vulnerable is viewed as a weakness and is often associated with a loss of masculinity. Male survivors of different forms of violence, as Sivakumaran (2007) argues, "are portrayed as passive, humiliated and indefinitely stripped of their manhood." Such a portrayal of male survivors as victims without a voice results in a disempowering "narrative of silenced, isolated, and wholly marginalized male survivors" devoid of their agency (Edström and Dolan, 2018). Few existing studies have problematized the underlying gendered assumptions of such portrayals and have instead discussed the agency of male survivors. Some have also highlighted the complexities of male agency in relation to the sociopolitical and gendered spaces in which it is exercised (Touquet and Schulz, 2020). Drawing from these studies and complexifying the binaries of victimhood and agency of former militants in Kashmir, I argue that it is, first, crucial to move beyond the projection of male victimhood as lost masculinity. Vulnerabilities of male survivors may not always imply a loss of manhood and the survivors of different forms of violence do not always perceive their vulnerabilities as a gender crisis. Second, vulnerabilities or victimhood of survivors coexist with the agency. Various scholars have questioned the "gendered opposition of agency and victimhood that typically characterizes the analysis of women's coping strategies in war zone" (Utas, 2005). Similarly, Krystalli (2020) succinctly articulates the need to incorporate a simultaneous analysis of victimhood and agency: "Taking victimhood seriously requires moving away from a view of it as always synonymous with vulnerability or lack of agency or as entirely reduced to the experience of victimization." Few studies have also extended this questioning to male agency and victimhood. Kreft and Schulz (2021) have similarly argued that a complex and intrinsic relationship exists between the victimhood and agency of male survivors of sexual violence in conflicts.

There is still a tendency to discuss the "going beyond/overcoming victimhood to becoming agents of change" for analysis of women survivors' victimhood and agency; and the study of the agency of male survivors of violence has not received as much attention in the Kashmir conflict. Through my interactions with survivors of physical/sexual violence in Kashmir, it is evident that there is no linear process or a "moment of arrival" of agency for the victims (both men and women). Navigating the experiences of violence and exercising agency is often a simultaneous and an interwoven process for the survivors. In line with the emerging scholarship on the complexities of agency of male survivors of violence, the discussion in chapter 4 shows that the agency of former militant men in Kashmir, for instance, is highly complex and their choices are shaped by the sociopolitical context and available spaces (in what Touquet and Schulz [2020] call the "opportunity structures"). In this regard, the case of Kashmir shows the different ways in which the survivors of both physical and sexual violence exercise their agency and navigate their victimizing experiences: through engagement with civil society, informal discussion/ chats with fellow survivors; and at the same time silence/nondisclosure, which is discussed later.

REFERENCES

Aboim, Sofia. *Plural Masculinities: The Remaking of the Self in Private life.* Farnham, UK: Ashgate. 2010.

Akbar, M. J. *Behind the Vale*. New Delhi: Roli Books. 2002.

Baweja, Harinder. "Kashmir: A Calculated Gamble." *India Today*. April 30, 1992.

Bazaz, P. N. *The History of Struggle for Freedom in Kashmir*. Srinagar: Gulshan Books. 1954.

Beaseley, Chrisitine. "Rethinking Hegemonic Masculinity in a Globalising World." *Men and Masculinities*. Vol. 11, Issue 1, 2008: 86–103.

Behera, Navnita. C. *Demystifying Kashmir*. Washington: The Brookings Institution. 2006.

Bulmer, Sarah & Eichler, Maya. "Unmaking Militarized Masculinity: Veterans and the Project of Military-to-Civilian Transition." *Critical Military Studies*. Vol. 2, Issue 2, 2017:161–81.

Connell, R. W. *Masculinities*. Cambridge, UK: Polity Press. 1995.

Connell, R. W. & Messerschmidt, James. "Hegemonic Masculinity: Rethinking the Concept." *Gender and Society*. Issue 19, 2005: 829–59.

Demetriou, Demetrakis Z. "Connell's Concept of Hegemonic Masculinity: A Critique." *Theory and Society*. Vol. 30, Issue 3, 2001: 337–61.

Duncanson, Claire. "Hegemonic Masculinity and the Possibility of Change in Gender Relations." *Men and Masculinities*. Vol. 18, Issue 2, 2015: 231–48.

Duriesmith, David. "Hybrid Warriors and the Formation of New War Masculinities: A Case Study of Indonesian Foreign Fighters." *Journal of Security and Development*. Vol.7, Issue 1, 2018: 1–16.

Duriesmith, David, and Ismail N. H. "Militarized Masculinities Beyond Methodological Nationalism of an Indonesian Jihadi." *International Theory*. Issue 11, 2019: 139–59.

Edström Jerker, and Dolan Chris. "Breaking the spell of silence: Collective healing as activism amongst refugee male survivors of sexual violence in Uganda." *Journal of Refugee Studies*. Vol. 32, Issue 2, 2018: 175–96.

Eriksson, Baaz, M., and Stern, M. *Sexual Violence as a Weapon of War? Perceptions, Prescriptions, Problems in the Congo and Beyond*. London: Zed Books, 2013.

Farman Ali, Rao. *Kashmir Under the Shadow of Gun: Making of Alfatah*. New Delhi: Uppal Publishing House. 2012.

Flood, Michael. "Between Men and Masculinity: An Assessment of the term 'Masculnity' in Recent Scholarship on Men." Pearce, Sharyn and Muller, Vivienne (eds.) *Manning the next Millennium: Studies in Masculinities*. Perth: Black Swan. 2002.

Ganguly, Sumit. "Explaining the Kashmir Insurgency: Political Mobilization and Institutional Decay." *International Security*. Vol. 21, Issue 2, 1996: 76–107.

Gardiner, Judith K. "Men, Masculinities, and Feminist Theory." Kimmel, Michael, Hearn, Jeff and Connell R. W. (eds.) *Handbook of Studies on Men & Masculinities*. Thousand Oaks, CA and London: Sage. 2005.

Gockhami, Abdul Jabbar. *Politics of Plebiscite*. Srinagar: Gulshan Publishers: 2007.

Gray, H., and Stern, M. "Risky Dis/entanglements: Torture and Sexual Violence in Conflict." *European Journal of International Relations*. Vol. 25, Issue 4, 2019: 1035–1058.

Habibullah, Wajahat. *My Kashmir: Conflict and the Prospects for Enduring Peace.* United States Institute for Peace Press. 2008.

Hollander, Theo. "Men, Masculinities, and the Demise of a State: Examining Masculinities in the Context of Economic, Political and Social Crisis in a Small Town in the Democratic Republic of the Congo." *Men and Masculinities.* Vol. 17, Issue 4, 2014: 417–39.

Kasturi, Malvika, and Mekhola Gomes. "Debate: History, Historians, and the Many Ideas of India: A Reply to Shonaleekha Kaul." *The Wire.* August 28, 2020.

Kaul, Shonaleekha. *The Making of Early Kashmir: Landscape and Identity in the Rajatarangini.* New Delhi: Oxford University Press. 2018.

Khan, Nyla Ali. *The Life of a Kashmiri Woman: Dialectic of Resistance and Accommodation.* New York: Palgrave Macmillan. 2014.

Khan, Rehman Hafizur. "Abdullah's Release and Re-arrest." *Pakistan Horizon.* Vol. 11, Issue 2, 1958: 99–109.

Kimmel, Michael. Integrating men into the curriculum. *Duke Journal of Gender, Law and Policy* 4, 1997. Available at: http://www.law.duke.edu/journals/djglp/articles/gen4p181.html (Accessed on 08/10/2020).

KL News Network. "1975 Accord changed J& K's Special Status: Sajad Lone" *Kashmir Life.* March 27, 2019. Available at: https://kashmirlife.net/1975-accord-changed-jks-special-status-sajad-lone-205643/.

Kreft, Anne-Katherine, and Schulz, P. "Beyond Passive Victims and Agentic Survivors: Responses to Conflict Related Sexual Violence." *E-International Relations.* 2021. Available at: https://www.e-ir.info/2021/04/03/beyond-passive-victims-and-agentic-survivors-responses-to-conflict-related-sexual-violence/ (Accessed on 06/04/21).

Krystalli, Roxani. "Women, Peace, and Victimhood." *IPI Global Observatory.* 2020. Available at: https://theglobalobservatory.org/2020/10/women-peace-and-victimhood/ (Accessed on 18/01/2021).

Leiby, Michele. "Digging in the Archives: The Promise and Perils of Primary Documents." *Politics & Society.* Vol. 37, No. 1, March 2009: 75–99.

Malik, Inshah. *Muslim Women, Agency, and Resistance Politics: The Case of Kashmir.* Switzerland: Palgrave Macmillan. 2019.

Moller, M. "Exploiting Patterns: A Critique of Hegemonic Masculinity." *Journal of Gender Studies.* Vol. 16. 2007: 263–76.

Morgan, David. "Theatre of War: Combat, the Military and Masculinities" in Harry Brod and Michael Kaufman (eds.) *Theorizing Masculinities.* London: Sage. 1994.

Myrttinen, Henri, Khattab L., and Naujoks J. "Re-thinking Hegemonic Masculinities in Conflict Affected Contexts." *Critical Military Studies.* Vol. 3, Issue 2, 2016: 103–19.

Noorani, A.G. *A Constitutional History of Jammu and Kashmir.* New Delhi: Oxford University Press. 2011.

Obrock, Luther. "Landscape in its Place: The Imagination of Kashmir in Sanskrit and Beyond." *History and Theory.* Vol. 59. Issue 1, 2020: 156–64.

Parashar, Swati. "Gender, Jihad and Jingoism: Women as Perpetrators, Planners, and Patrons of Militancy in Kashmir." *Studies in Conflict and Terrorism*. Vol. 34, Issue 4, 2011: 295–317.

Puri, Balraj. *Kashmir: Towards Insurgency*. New Delhi: Orient Longman. 1993.

Rai, Mridu. *Hindu Rulers, Muslim Subjects: Islam, Rights, and the History of Kashmir*. Princeton, NJ: Princeton University Press. 2004.

Schofield, Victoria. *Kashmir in Conflict: India, Pakistan, and the Unending War*. London & New York: I. B. Tauris. 2003.

Schulz, Philipp. *Male Survivors of Wartime Sexual Violence: Perspectives from Northern Uganda*. Oakland, California: University of California Press. 2020.

Sivakumaran, S. 2007. "Sexual Violence against Men in Armed Conflict." *European Journal of International Law*. Vol. 18, Issue 2, 2007: 253–76.

Sjoberg, L. and Gentry, C. *Mothers, Monsters, Whores: Women's Violence in Global Politics*. London/New York: Zed Books, 2007.

Theidon, Kimberly. "Reconstructing Masculinities: The Disarmament, Demobilization and Reintegration of Former Combatants in Colombia." *Human Rights Quarterly*. Issue 31, 2009: 1–31.

Thorp. Robert. *Kashmir Misgovernment* (edited). Srinagar: Gulshan Publishers. 2011.

Touquet, Heleen, and Schulz, Philipp. "Navigating Vulnerabilities and Masculinities: How Gendered Contexts Shape the Agency of Male Sexual Violence survivors." *Security Dialogue*. 2020. Available at: https://journals.sagepub.com/doi/full/10.1177/0967010620929176.

Utas, Mats. "Victimcy, Girlfiending, Soldiering: Tactic Agency in a Young Woman's Social Navigation of Liberian War Zone." *Anthropological Quarterly*, Vol. 78, Issue 2, 2005: 403–30.

Whitehead, Andrew. *A Mission in Kashmir*. London: Penguin Global. 2007.

Whitehead, Andrew. "Kashmir's Forgotten Women Militia." *The Wire*. 2017. Available at: https://thewire.in/gender/kashmir-women-militia.

Zalewski, Marysia. "What's the Problem with the Concept of Military Masculinity." *Critical Military Studies*. Vol.3, Issue 2, 2017: 200–5.

NOTES

1. Kashmiri Pandits are Kashmiri Hindus. The Brahmin Kashmiri Pandits claim to have lived in the North Indian mountainous region of Indian administered Kashmir for over 5,000 years. The term "pandit" is an honorable title, which means a wise man/scholar of Hinduism.

2. The UN Security Council Resolution 47 is available at: http://unscr.com/en/resolutions/doc/47 (Accessed on 30/03/21).

3. Schofield (2003) lists the following wings: The militant group Al Barq, had links with Abdul Gani Lone's People's Conference. Al Fateh, led by Zain-ul Abdeen, a former contestant in the 1987 elections, was the armed wing of one faction of Shabir Shah's People League. Another armed faction of People's League was Al-Jehad.

4. Personal Interview on 05/09/2015.

Chapter 3

Military Masculinities of the State Armed Forces in Kashmir

Military masculinity has been used as a significant concept by feminist IR scholars to examine male gender roles, performances, and embodiments in military and military-like institutions and organizations. In the South Asian feminist IR literature, efforts to show war and armed conflict as a masculine activity have successfully contributed toward highlighting the gendered nature of institutions like national security, where feminist voices are excluded. These significant efforts made by feminists are crucial in the study of gender, peace, and conflict. In this process, however, terms like "military masculinity," "hegemonic masculinity," or "hyper-masculinity" are used, most often in a singular, monolithic manner to highlight the violence of men. This leads to the reproduction and reinforcement of these terms "without relating them to their respective local, historical, political and socio-economic contexts" (Myrttinen, Khattab, and Naujoks, 2017).

The Critical Scholarship on Men and Masculinities (CSMM) and some feminist scholars have problematized the simplified usage of masculinity in conflict affected contexts and have also called upon a re-examining of the concepts associated with masculinity. The re-examination, or perhaps an in-depth study of masculinities—represented through behavior, perception, and practices—remains limited in the case of South Asian conflicts, although there are some important exceptions.[1] Using the case of Kashmir, I argue that there is a need to problematize the monolithic, and sometimes a less thoughtful use of masculinity in conflict-affected contexts. There are multiple masculinities in conflicts that often get overlooked in research, due to our focus on military/militarized violence. Even within the military masculinities, there are gender and other hierarchies that are often rendered invisible due to the dominant focus on the linkage between violence and military/militarized men.

In this chapter, I propose to extend our understanding of military masculinity, from an idealized and violent way of being a man in conflicts, to also a space where men make sense of their gender identity in relation to the hegemonic narratives of masculinity. To reach a more nuanced assessment of military masculinity, it is important to ask questions like these: "How do military men perceive manhood?" "Which traits and characteristics are entailed in this perception?" "What practices and methods of military life facilitate their advancement toward achieving their perceived ideals of manhood?" "How do their masculinities intersect with dominant religious and nationalist narratives?" Military and combat are important factors that shape violent masculinities in conflict. However, by focusing only on violence, we let go of the potential to engage with the process of masculinization of men and institutions. Such an engagement can provide a deeper understanding of military as a gendered institution. In the same light, this chapter addresses and engages with the perceived meanings of military masculinities through the interviews of Indian army personnel (retired and working) in Kashmir.

This chapter is broadly divided into three sections. The first engages with the idealized elements of the military masculinity, as outlined in the existing feminist IR literature. In short, how military masculinity is considered as the ideal/ hegemonic type of masculinity in conflict affected regions. In the second section, the chapter explores the ideal type of military masculinity in the context of Kashmir; along with its intersections with Hindutva[2] and nationalist politics. The third section, on the one hand, primarily focuses on the interviews of army personnel, and on the other, popular cultural practices to understand perceptions of manhood, possible gaps in performativity, and reproduction of gendered behavior. In the end, the chapter concludes by discussing the connection between these three sections: the focus on the idealized masculinity of military men, their perceptions of manhood, and their actual lived experiences.

IDEALIZED MILITARY MASCULINITIES

[W]hen the normativity of the soldier, military, state, and empire are lined up such that the cleansing of the troops purifies the other entities simultaneously. . . . Accordingly, constructions of the soldier's toughness, masculinity, dominance, heterosexuality, and stoicism can conjure images of military strength, state, legitimacy, and imperial righteousness, while depictions of the soldier's flaws can implicate notions of military weakness and state and imperial illegitimacy. (Belkin, 2012)

Feminist literature on militarism has identified the realm of international security as being dominated by masculine-coded values and norms. These norms in international politics are particularly evident in militarized institutions and serve as a path by which masculine states and men can prove their manliness.[3] This is because militarism has long been understood as an extension of the male body, and when nations rely upon their militaries to defend themselves, it builds strong links between the military, soldiers, and the nation. Hooper (2001) points out that the idealized masculinity for soldiers serving in military have throughout history included characteristics associated with aggression, bravery, courage, service, precision, and protection. In the same context, Stephen Wicks (1996) wrote that the "warrior, foremost among male archetypes . . . has been the epitome of masculinity in many societies. A man learns to deny all that is 'feminine' and soft in himself." The pressure on any state's military to live up to these idealized masculine characteristics, is mentioned in Goldstein's (2001) work as "the act of military service forced men to enact rites of passage (practice) into artificial manhood (ideal)." Similarly, Peterson (2010) also argues that the edifice of masculinity is a mythic creation, the pressure to prove one's manhood is relentless. This pressure is particularly acute on the stage of political and military power because the stakes are high, especially in the context of succeeding in an impending war or conflict.

To understand why the state militaries are intrinsically masculine, it's helpful to draw upon Enloe's (2004) idea of masculinization. She argues that masculinization often is fuelled by key players' anxieties and fears of feminization; that there are those who worry that if they are perceived to be "feminine" that they will lose political influence, credibility, or respect and are likely to take steps to avoid being perceived that way. "They will stay quiet about their genuine reservations; they might speak publicly about the values of strength and decisive threatening action, they will make clear that they are personally always ready to wield the military might; they might even cast doubt on the manliness of those who are criticising military solutions" (Enloe, 2004). She also points out how the process of masculinization is most evident in the state structures, which in turn further promotes militaristic solutions and awards the politically valuable label "manly" to those who define security in militarized terms.

It is not surprising then to see the reluctance of the armies across the globe to allow women in a masculinized space. This can be explained in view of the fact that state military institutions promote patriarchy, which can best survive and thrive if its leaders and members can perpetuate a widely accepted standard of "proper" femininity. In doing so, they can manage to make "femininity" appear as natural and, not a product of human decisions. If they can achieve this, then the entire patriarchal order is likely to take on the status of "natural" and not be challenged in a fundamental way. Furthermore, by introducing more women in spaces thus far exclusively reserved for men, it becomes difficult to sustain the seeming naturalness of the dichotomy between masculinity and femininity, which may become a major threat to notions of hegemonic masculinity. So, these institutions profess "natural" justifications to keep out the femininity.

Cohn (2000) explores the aversion of military men toward gender integration in military. Through the interviews of officers in the US military, she argues that physical training is a dominant form through which male officers frame their opposition to women in military. The difference in the standards of physical training for women is often used as a significant argument for their incapacity to join combat or intense military activities. These arguments, as Cohn shows in her paper, also point toward men's anxieties and feelings of loss and anger toward changes in the way the organization is gendered. Such anxieties that manifest in public arguments against women in military and in combat are not just restricted to the United States. Similar arguments are made in the rest of the world. These are also starkly visible in the case of the Indian Army that has followed a strategic policy of noninduction of women in combat arms. This official policy helps men maintain their position of dominance over women. Although, recently in 2021, there were some reports suggesting plans to move women soldiers to combat roles in the Indian state armed Forces. For instance, in July 2021 there were reports of women soldiers from the Assam Rifles (paramilitary force) deployed in Kashmir to assist the armed forces "to assist Indian troops in maintaining peace" (Press Trust of India, 2021). Photographs of them in their combat gears and guns while frisking Kashmiri women were widely circulated. Their role is however, still seen within the gendered parameters—to bridge the gap between locals and armed forces and as Mushtaq (2021) writes, their position is constructed in opposition to the "other"—"the dangerous Kashmiri muslim women radicalised by the Kashmiri muslim men, potential threats to the idea of India and thus, need to be put in place." It is interesting how different womens' position and identities are constructed differently in the military discourse to serve the patriarchal ends of the institution. Women, in the military institutions mostly work as Short Service Commission (SSC) and Permanent Regular Commission (PRC) officers in medical, dental, and nursing services. In an article written by a retired army officer Suman (2010), shares his opinion on whether women should be inducted for combat role in the Army, he insists that

> defence matters cannot be treated as publicity gimmick to flaunt sexual equality. Decisions taken as a matter of political and populist expediency can prove disastrous for the Nation in the long run . . . Women's expertise, talent and competence should be profitably utilized in areas which are totally non-combat in nature. For the present, women must continue to play their established role in the medical, dental and nursing services, both as SSC and PRC officers.

However, they should not be granted SSC in any other branch. The current policy of non-induction of women in combat arms should continue. (Suman, 2010)

While discussing the limitations of considering women for combat roles, similar arguments regarding physical fitness and training surface in Indian military circles, too:[4]

Standards of physical fitness of women can never be the same as those of men. It is a biological reality and is true for all fields including sports. In the case of women officers, Indian army has lowered the standards to appallingly low levels. Even then many women fail to qualify during their pre-commission training. Whereas male cadets are required to run 5 km in 28 minutes, women are given 40 minutes. Similarly, males are required to jump across a 9 feet wide ditch with full equipment and personal weapon; women have to negotiate only a 5 feet wide ditch. Worse, most women fail in the test.

All male officers and soldiers are subjected to annual battle physical efficiency tests till they attain the age of 45 years. No such tests have been prescribed for women officers to avoid embarrassment to them in front of the troops. Concerns have also been expressed about the susceptibility of Indian women to frequent back problems, pelvic injuries and stress fractures. A recent review conducted by the British Army concluded that women have neither the upper-body strength nor the physical resilience to withstand intensive combat.

The prospect of inclusion of women in masculinized spaces increases male anxieties and as a result, essentialist logic, and justification of biological differences are used to reassert the gender binaries. In another such interview, an army officer from Kashmir, argued this:

Women around the world are not deployed in combat operations. A large number of women are deployed in Iraq and Afghanistan but their role is limited to support functions. This is simply because, firstly, women cannot be assigned many duties such as night duties, they are not as physically fit as men to fight enemies and induction of women officers or soldiers gives an impression of the *environment being softer leading to disastrous results for national security.* Also, according to Israeli studies, when females are inducted for combat roles, the soldiers first instinct is to save the women in their military ranks rather than fighting against the enemy. (emphasis added)[5]

It is paradoxical, though, because while the Indian army officers stress upon the physical incapacity of women to stop them from being inducted in the combat, they import some of the best artillery and armor used in combat from the world, which does not require much physical strength for operational purposes. For instance, during the Kargil war, the Indian Army imported advanced weaponry such as grenade launchers, satellite

surveillance, battlefield radars, mine proof vehicles, unmanned aerial vehicles, and frequency hoppers for the combat operations that do not require
much physical competence (Chengappa, 1999). Discouraging women from
performing combat roles on different pretexts clearly shows that the army and
the other state militarized forces want the space of combat remain masculine
and deter any signs of femininity to encroach upon this space. This is true of
most of the state armies across the world where it is a standard practice to
keep the women out of combat zones. However, with more recent discussions
and plans to move towards inclusion of women in combat roles, in the Indian
Armed Forces, the difference is yet to be seen.

The clear demarcation of the binaries of masculine and feminine also
facilitates the masculinist protection imaginaries—where a good soldier protects the nation and its people. The nation is called up in familial language:
motherland, kin, blood, home. As Pettman (1996) asserts, the state is often
the gendered male and the nation gendered female; the mother country. The
citizen/children become the kin. The nationalist discourse represents the
nation as the mother whose honor must be defended by the soldier-son. Such
themes lead to ideas of supreme sacrifices. Husbands, lovers, and sons can be
lost forever for the sake of protecting the nation/mother (Khattak, 1997). This
is visible in Elshtain's (1987) description of the good soldier and the good
mother–while the good soldier protects the mother nation, a good mother
is ready to sacrifice her son for the cause of the nation. Similar gendered
representations are extensively researched in post-colonial contexts as well.
A number of post-colonial critics have explained, for instance, how female
bodies and sexuality have been appropriated in Indian nationalist discourses.
The work of Chatterjee (1993), for example, shows how the Indian woman's
body acts as the symbolic representation of motherland.

> The construction of motherhood in this discourse emerged as an articula-
> tion of the conventional worship of mother goddesses (mata), embodying the
> fundamental creative sexual power (shakti), protecting their human flock,
> with the new construction of the "Indian Woman" in the emerging nationalist
> middle-class cultures in the major cities as a supreme sign of the nation, of the
> inner spiritual realm marked by devotion and purity in which the woman was
> mother and goddess. (Chatterjee, 1993)

This imagery of the nation as mother also has a significant role to play in
the creation of the idealized military masculinity represented by the Indian
state armed forces (discussed in more detail in chapter 5). Indian army in
their physical training sessions often invoke slogans of Mother India to motivate the soldiers. Following words of an Indian soldier further explains this
sentiment:

I have seen many dead bodies. Initially I used to feel so sick, but now I am used to it. Being in the army I have become fearless. I am not scared of death anymore. Our training in the army is such that it makes us brave. Even if I die, I will be satisfied dying for my *motherland*, which is an honour.[6]

Similarly, a retired army officer who served in Kashmir during the peak of the militancy remarked,

Being posted in Kashmir is an extremely stressful proposition. However, an army officer who is posted in Kashmir has in front of him the best opportunity to serve his country. Since it is a troubled region, he will have lot of chances to prove his love for *Mother India*. But along with it he has a tremendous responsibility of protecting his mother from the enemies. It is not easy. You cannot even imagine the stress and trauma that comes along with it.[7]

The physical discipline along with aggressive training, creates feelings of bravery and courage among the soldiers. They are taught to work hard with determination in order to serve Mother India by fighting against its enemies. The army training also involves shouting aloud slogans of victory, bravery, and determination to motivate themselves. For instance, in a training camp, when the soldiers got down from a tank and crawled down tunnels under barbed wires, they had to reach the dummies of the enemies and shoot them, at which point, they all shouted together, "Bharat Mata ki Jai" (praise and glory to mother India), which motivated them to quickly reach and shoot.[8] When asked about such tactics, the officer in command replied saying, "these are methods to keep the soldiers motivated. After so much physical strain, the body feels weak, but the passion to serve the mother nation reenergizes the soldier."[9]

The logic of the masculinist protection offered by Young (2003) is quite relevant to understand the symbolic representations of the "brave soldier" and "mother nation." As Young argues, in the gendered logic of masculinist protection, the masculine protector puts those protected (paradigmatically women and children) in a subordinate position of dependence and obedience. This logic can be extended to the operations of the security state in war and conflicts; and at the micro level it can be seen as projected through the brave soldiers. The imagery of the good/ brave soldier is opposed to "the dominant man who desires sexual capture of women," which, according to Young (2003, 4–5), is a benign masculinity, associated more with the ideas of chivalry:

The gallantly masculine man is loving and self-sacrificing, especially in relation to women. He faces the world's difficulties and dangers in order to shield women from harm . . . The role of this courageous, responsible and virtuous man is that of a protector.

The feminine woman, rather, on this construction, adores her protector and happily defers to his judgment in return for the promise of security that he offers. She looks up to him with gratitude for his manliness and admiration for his willingness to face the dangers of the world for her sake.

The above construction of the idealized masculinity of the soldier is toward the protected—the weak and vulnerable. In return for his protection, the subordinate citizens provide their obedience and loyalty. For the outside world, however, he is expected to be a violent, aggressive, and a duty-bound soldier who is always prepared to defend his country against an aggressor. Both these external and internal roles of the soldier are built upon a direct contrast to the feminine qualities. The military masculinity (represented by the security state, military men, and state military institutions), through its clearly laid out differences from the feminine and the use of the gendered logic of masculinist protection, becomes the idealized masculinity in contexts of conflict. In the following two sections, I explore the multiple layers and intersections involved in the enactment of the military masculinity both in the mainland India and more specifically in Kashmir. The discussion is grounded in the local, sociopolitical, and religious context to understand how the masculinity of military men is shaped and venerated. Also, the cultural practices that glorify this masculinity and finally how military men make sense of their manhood in relation to the idealized forms of masculinity.

IDEALIZED MILITARY MASCULINITY IN INDIA: INTERSECTIONS AND REPRESENTATIONS

The military masculinity of the state armed forces in Kashmir cannot be understood in isolation from the ongoing Hindutva politics and the right-wing nationalist discourse in mainland India. The Bhartiya Janata Party's (BJP) coming to power in 2014 has resulted in the assertion of a new Hindu identity, which, as Anand (2007) argues, conflates nationalism with masculinity and violence. The Hindutva masculinity is built upon postcolonial nation-building anxieties and also through invocation of a fictional inimical figure of the dangerous Muslim "other," which is "a mix of negative images of Islam, history, physicality, and culture" (Anand, 2007). Similarly, Parashar (2018) talks of both postcolonial anxieties and a crisis of masculinity as contributing toward the Hindutva moment in Indian politics:

India's postcolonial anxiety is (re)produced in popular histories of colonialism and its legacy in public discourses, relived through everyday collective memories. The crisis of masculinity, on the other hand, is manifested in the rejection of a feminized/androgynous/soft Indian state in the post-independence Gandhi-Nehru era (1947–64), and the invocation of the great ancient pre-Islamic Indian past, when Hindu men shaped their culture and destiny alongside exercising patriarchal control over "their" women.

Hindu nationalism is mainly embodied within various political and cultural organizations, which are together called the Sangh Parivar (Sangh family). BJP is the main political party associated with it, Rashtriya Swayamsevak Sangh (RSS) [National Volunteer Organization] provides the ideological foundation and other members include Vishwa Hindu Parishad (VHP), Bajrang Dal, Rashtriya Sevika Samiti, and Durga Vahini. The RSS entails military practices and training of young men who perform physical exercises and martial training with long sticks (lathis). They recite their oath of commitment toward the regeneration of a pure Hindu nation, standing in rows while their hands are stretched in front of their chest. Another Hindutva promoting regional party "Shiv Sena" (Maratha warrior king Shivaji's army) also adopts military practices and sometimes emulation of the supposed militant Muslim practices. Hansen (1996) shows in his detailed exploration of the recuperation of masculinity (Hindu potency)—a common theme in both these organizations is achieved through the othering of Muslims and physical activism along with discipline. The Hindu nationalist discourse is also based on the gendered representation of the nation as Hindu mother—an object of worship, reverence, and protection—clearly articulated in Bankim Chattopadhyay image of Bharat Mata (Mother India).[10]

In the contemporary surge of Hindu nationalist sentiments in India, Hindutva has gained legitimacy and is naturalized as a norm. When the Hindu nationalist politics is embraced by the state institution, it can prove to be hostile for the non-Hindu minorities (Anand, 2007). In this context, the masculinized Hindu nationalist discourse has serious implications in Kashmir valley, which has a majority of Muslim inhabitants. Advocates of Hindutva view the Kashmiri struggle for self-determination as a threat to the sovereignty and integrity of the Hindu nation (Parashar, 2018). In mainland India, people criticizing violence, human rights violations, and abrogation of Article 370 in Kashmir are sometimes considered as harming the national interest. The heavy militarization along with the surge of Hindu nationalist sentiments in India has further added to the hostile situation in Kashmir. The counterinsurgency operations have also been influenced by the contemporary political context in India.

As opposed to the Hindu military practices, the state armed forces—especially the Indian army—emphasize an intergroup harmony, internally, wherein all officers, junior commissioned and jawans *(soldiers)* take part in celebration of all religions represented in a unit. Religious teachers including Pandits, Maulwis, and granthis (representing Hindu, Muslim, and Sikh religions) all impart their particular religious teachings, but concerning other faiths. On the surface, the military institutions follow a strict secular code of conduct and appear highly Indianized. However, certain internal practices and symbolism do highlight a subtle religious bias. Khalidi (2001/2), for instance in his work on ethnic group recruitment in the Indian army in 2002, discussed emerging problems of overlapping nationalist and Hindu values in the military. Here, he provided examples such as refusal to permit Friday prayers (an Islamic religious obligation to be performed in congregation), and refusal to allow Muslim soldiers to grow beards as compared to Sikh soldiers. Another example is the invitation to politicians from RSS and Shiv Sena to military events. Also, distribution of *Rakhis* (Hindu sacred wristbands given by women to men as a token of sisterly love and a promise to protect their sisters) to the jawans by Vishva Hindu Parishad, which is an anti-Christian and anti-Muslim organization, also highlight some practices that subtly favor Hinduism. (Khalidi, ibid).

The representations of an idealized masculinity of military men with a subtle Hindu characterization are also widespread in contemporary Bollywood movies starring actors like Akshay Kumar, who is considered to be the ideal modern patriot. The media has a significant role in perpetuating the intimate connection between the Indian army and the idealized masculine characteristics of heroism, patriotism, violence, and aggression, on the one hand, and loving, caring protector on the other. Movies made about wars that involve the Indian army serve as an important medium in idealizing the army's masculine nature and circulating this as a "natural" and "good" phenomenon. Such depictions help in justifying the infliction of violence on the one hand, and on the other hand, it also encourages young men from different parts of the country to join the army or idolize the men in the army. For example, young boys in the metropolitan cities of India idolize the actors who act as army men in the movies. A popular hairdresser in a famous salon in New Delhi noted that "men mostly like a crew cut, something like Akshay Kumar's (an Indian actor who plays the role of a soldier in many movies) haircut in the movie *Holiday*."[11] Similarly, men aspire to have strong bodies like the army heroes depicted in the movies. A common conversation with the boys who regularly go to the gym, shows they are driven to build their bodies just like the people in the army "who are strong and fit; they are able to fight enemies and they are able to protect their country or their mothers and sisters in crisis."[12]

There are also Bollywood movies that portray the Indian army's role in Kashmir, some examples are *Prahaar, Border, LOC Kargil,* and *Lakshya.* These popular movies can be seen as important exemplars used to idolize the militaristic characteristics and the creation of an idealized masculinity of the Indian army. For instance, the movie *Prahaar* shows the training process of the jawans (soldiers) in the army. Major Chouhan's character is tasked with training a few soldiers through aggressive training methods. It is through vigorous training that the young soldiers are taught to be disciplined and make the transition from "a boy to a man." Similarly, *Lakshya* also depicts the story of a young college-going boy, Karan, who has no ambition in his life and who joins the army, following his friend. After joining the army and going through a vigorous training, however, this boy learns to be disciplined and achieves the ideals of masculinity such as bravery, violence, and aggression.

Movies such as *Border* and *LOC Kargil,* on the other hand, show how the army's main duty is perceived to be the protection of Mother India. There is a line of dialogue in the movie where one army officer asks another, "Why we kill an enemy, even though he is another mother's son?" and the other officer responds:

> If you don't kill him, he will kill you and trample upon your motherland's bare chest. We have never looked at someone's mother with bad intentions. But we are not such cowards that we will let anyone look at our mother with a dirty eye and we don't do anything about it. No! Never!

Use of force, violence, and aggression interwoven with patriotism, bravery, and heroism are reflected in the movies revolving around the role of Indian army in serving the nation. They also show how being a man is equivalent to being aggressive and being able to protect the nation from the enemies. For instance, in the movie *Border*, an Indian army major talks to the Pakistani army and tells them this:

> Mard hai toh Saamne aa, Fir tumhe pata chalega ki Maj. Kuldeep Singh, mard hai ya nahi,
>
> (If you are a man then come show me your face, then you will get to know whether I [Maj. Kuldeep Singh] am a man or not)

Similarly, a dialogue in the movie *LOC Kargil* also links bravery to expectations of masculinity:

> Musibaton se bhaagna nahi, balki inka saamna karna mardon ka kaam hai
>
> (Not running away from problems, but facing them bravely is the job of men)

Such portrayals made by cinema leave a significant impact on the male youth of the country as they relate manhood with such portrayals. They idolize these characteristics and attempt to emulate them. Bollywood plays a significant role in creating imagined ideal masculinities. Military masculinity in India has taken different forms which are not only represented by Indian army personnel but also young men belonging to the Hindu nationalist organizations such as RSS, Shiv Sena, and Bajrang Dal that preach ideals of discipline and physical training. The modern middle class Indian young men, however, idolize the masculinity of the modern soldier who is portrayed as physically fit, patriotic, heroic, and at the same time loving, caring, and protective toward women. The next section, through the lived experiences of army officers and soldiers, explores their actual perception of manhood in relation to the discussed idealized traits of military masculinity.

STATE MILITARY MEN IN KASHMIR: EXPECTATIONS, PERCEPTIONS, AND LIVED EXPERIENCES

As discussed in previous sections, the idealized masculinity represented by the state military entails characteristics of bravery, courage, patriotism, heroism, protection, and sacrifice. An army recruitment advertisement in Kashmir explicitly mentions that the basic duty of the army is to protect the integrity of the nation through ideals like service, sacrifice, and patriotism:

> The army offers outstanding career opportunities to the *courageous* young candidates. It is a career that offers enormous facilities, a privileged lifestyle and above all, honour in serving the country. The Armed Forces characterize *the ideals of service, sacrifice, patriotism* and our country's composite culture. The basic duty of the Army is *to safeguard the territorial integrity of the nation* against external aggression. The Army is often required to support the civil administration during internal security disturbances and in the maintenance of law and order. (emphasis added)[13]

Similarly, Sam Manekshaw's[14] quote, which is hung on the walls of army camps, explicitly showed that the qualities of a good soldier were opposite to those of a saint or a mahatma:

> He who neither drinks, nor smokes, nor dances; He who preaches and even occasionally practices piety, tolerance and celibacy, is generally a saint, or a Mahatma or more likely a humbug but he certainly won't make a leader or for that matter a good soldier.[15]

This quote conveys a strong distinction between a saint and a good soldier in order to strongly project the masculinity of the good soldier. The use of the phrase, "He is more likely a humbug," shows the rejection of the association of being masculine with saintly qualities like celibacy, temperance, and piety. Such symbols, icons, and private media's depictions of men in the military, embodies all of the qualities of the hegemonic male that makes a national hero, giving further meaning and importance to men who imbibe such qualities. By doing so, these qualities strengthen their hold on the parameters of manhood. Also, by appealing to ideal images of masculine power and control, the military creates an unproblematized image of military service and warfare, winning the hearts and minds of Indians, and encouraging men to wilfully and enthusiastically participate.

How far do the state military men in Kashmir live up to these idealized forms of military masculinity in India? How do they really perceive manhood in relation to the expected way of being a man, and how can we rethink the concept of military masculinity through the actual lived experiences of soldiers and military men? These are some questions that I pose and attempt to address in the next section. This is important in order to revisit military masculinities through an experiential lens and understand the nuances, instead of simplistically attributing military masculinity as violence of men. To understand different perceptions of manhood, I interviewed jawans (soldiers) regarding their physical and weapons training; along with the officers involved in counterinsurgency operations. Also, later in the section, I discuss some slogans and engravings on army camps as important indicators of a trend to throw masculine challenges at the Kashmiri insurgents and supporters of militancy.

Physical Training

Like militaries across the globe, vigorous physical and weapon training is a part of military practices in the Indian army. In the 1990s, when the insurgency was growing rapidly, Indian armed forces were required to intensify their counterinsurgency operations in Kashmir. The various military and paramilitary units operating in Kashmir include the Border Security Force (BSF), the Central Reserve Police Force (CRPF), and the Rashtriya Rifles (RF) who work in conjunction with the special counterterrorism task forces of the state police, such as the Special Task Force (STF) and Special Operations Group (SOG). Since the mid-1990s, the army has installed a three-tiered counter-infiltration system along the Line of Control (LoC) and International Border (IB). The first tier was on the border itself and aimed to intercept and kill any insurgents trying to enter from Pakistan. Constant patrolling and ambushes were mounted to check infiltration. The second tier consisted of a five-kilometer-long belt from the border. There was a night curfew in this belt, with shoot-to-kill orders. The third tier was to conduct "cordon and search" villages behind the five-kilometer belt. Depending on the area, the size of these tiers varied. For example, in the Kupwara sector, the second tier could include an area up to 15 kilometers or more (Kasturi, 2012; Swami, 2011; Subramaniam, 2000). The counterinsurgency operations are not fixed and evolve constantly, changing in intensity in accordance with the changing requirements. An army officer who had been actively involved in the counter insurgency operations in the 1990s noted,

> These men (militants) understand only one language. That is force. In the 1990s when the insurgency was at its peak, we had to develop more lethal strategies on the border to deter the infiltrators. Although Indian Army has been success-ful in countering insurgency; and sometimes we are required to shoot, and if we didn't, they would go about saying that the Army got scared of them.[16]

Orders, such as to shoot-to-kill and cordon and search operations, enable the state to control and dominate any force that challenges the state hegemony. Furthermore, the Indian army officers are endowed with extraordinary pow-ers through the Armed Forces Special Powers Act (AFSPA). This act was applied to Kashmir in 1990, and permits army officers to arrest without a war-rant, search any vehicle, shoot to kill, and receive immunity from persecution. Due to the impunity under the act, "Indian Armed Forces have used severe forms of intimidation-torture, extrajudicial killings, disappearances, kidnap-ping and rape—to curb resistance" (Batool and Rather, 2016). Kashmiri and international human rights organizations have documented cases of human rights violations committed by the Indian Armed forces. AFSPA has, to a large extent, resulted in establishing dominance of military in Kashmir. Despite the exceptional powers bestowed upon the Indian army and regular reports of human rights violations, the insurgency along with popular resis-tance has continued to grow in Kashmir.

The year 2008 marked the intensification of street protests, especially stone-throwing (Kak, 2017) which resulted in further stringent and often repressive counterstrategies by the state. Street resistance in the form of stone-throwing is met by weapons and methods like pellet guns and firing. Alongside that, the Indian state has formed strategic alliances with coun-tries like Israel for counterterrorism. In this alliance, both the states—India and Israel—are fairly attentive to the similarities between the Kashmiri and Palestinian contexts, and their strong strategic partnership and cooperation on counterterrorism are primarily driven by that understanding. After the revoca-tion of Kashmir's autonomous status and territorial sovereignty, some collab-orative events between India and Israel highlight the overlapping ideology of

Israeli and Hindutva forces against the same perceived enemy. (Pandit, 2019). Along with being the top buyer of Israeli arms and also spyware, India also participates in joint counterterrorism military exercises with Israel. Indian special forces trained by Israel are then deployed in India's Northern territories including Kashmir (Pandit, 2019). Most of the recent military tactics to quell Kashmiri resistance are largely learned from Israel.

The Indian army and other military forces involved in the counterinsurgency operations go through extensive training in harsh conditions to prepare their cadre and to make "men out of boys" for fighting the militants. For instance, a COIN (counterinsurgency) warfare school was created by the Indian army in Khrew in 1994. It was equipped with firing ranges, an IED (improvised explosive device). Detection and training center, and a mock-up of an entire Kashmir village. All army units to be deployed in the COIN operations in Kashmir were sent to this school for training. The warfare school in Sonmarg also involves difficult training for the soldiers (Ganguly and Fidler, 2009). Indian troops are vigorously trained to operate in mountainous terrains, conduct cordon and search operations, cross rivers, crawl under barbed wires, climb up walls made of tires, walk on ropes, cross extremely narrow bridges, and so on.

More recently, the corps battle warfare school in Sarol provides ground to conduct specialized training to all units inducted into 16 Corps Zone. The 16 Corps Zone, according to an army officer (in 2016), "had become an active ground for militant operations and a large number of troops being involved in counterinsurgency and countermilitancy operations, a need was felt to have an organization which could train troops for the role in the new environment."[17] Around 24,000 to 30,000 troops are trained annually. Training includes challenging battle drills, tactical exercises, training movies, and firing practices, along with extensive counter IED neutralising training.[18] The military men who were and are involved in counterinsurgency operations acknowledge the arduous nature of training required for countering insurgency and resistance. However, they also consider the training as an opportunity to achieve manhood. The perception of manhood, however, differs according to the military ranks and hierarchies. Commanding officers, for instance, feel accomplished when they are able to train and discipline battalions/units. As a commanding officer of a battalion puts it,

> Being in the Army you become a man. You have to wake up before sun rise. Go through extensive physical training, drill, climb up difficult terrains, get your clothes dirty and so on. Not everybody can do this. Not everybody can be so disciplined. That is why we are proud to be in the Army. It is only through regular hard work and determination; we are able to create a battalion that is ready to fight insurgency.[19]

Jawans and soldiers in the lower ranks, on the other hand, associate manhood with disciplined maturity that comes through challenging physical and
weapons training.[20] Being physically fit, disciplined, putting in hard work,
and determination are supposed to be the characteristics of an ideal military
man, and militarized institutions provide the platform that ostensibly provides
legitimacy to express such manhood. Another soldier explained it like this:

> My uniform is a part of me. I feel satisfied when I have had a day full of physical
> training. When I go home, I feel a strong sense of manhood. It is not only because
> of what I do here, but also how people look at me, with respect and awe.[21]

In most interviews, the soldiers displayed patriotic sentiments and perceived
manhood in relation to their disciplining army practices and weapons.
Soldiering in the form of training practices and combat, however, does not
solely assert manhood—the respect and status they earn in their homes and
civilian societies completes the feeling. There are, however, some exceptions too. An interesting account of a soldier shows his tacit disillusionment
toward becoming a soldier. He explained that on joining the army, he was
very enthusiastic to live a military lifestyle and train in weapons, however, as
time went on, he felt disillusioned. Throughout his career, he had witnessed
violence and at times felt disconnected from the purpose, but carried on due
to a sense of duty:

> It is not a good feeling to encounter violence. I have seen a lot of blood, which
> sometimes makes me wonder. Those are moments when I deeply question what
> and why we are doing what we do. But those are only few moments. I am not
> so enthusiastic about guns and violence as I used to be when I was younger. But
> those are some phases, we feel as human beings. As a soldier, I feel my biggest
> duty is to serve my country.[22]

The tremendous pressure to live up to the military mindset and masculine
practices, sometimes leads to moments of introspection among the soldiers.
The violence that they see closely, results in some questioning and contemplation. Such reflexive behavior of military men is also important to study
the gap between the expectations of masculine behaviour and their real lived
experiences. Reflexivity has emotional connotations and may be considered
less masculine, but by reinforcing military masculinity as a violent category,
we leave out the scope for highlighting such nuances and complexities. To
understand their perspective on emotions, I asked two senior retired officers
about their feelings on violent encounters and if they ever regretted the
use of violence. Both of them acknowledged the emotional discomfort and
stress that results due to the extreme nature of their jobs, especially when
posted in challenging regions. One even mentioned the emotional upheaval

after combat and each violent encounter. However, the perceived feelings of "patriotism and righteousness of path" seem to act as a "balm to the emotional wounds in the job."[23]

> The emotional pain that one goes through while performing our jobs can be excruciating but we overcome it through determination and resolve, that we cultivate through difficult training and discipline. Being an Army man is not about being unemotional and indifferent, but it is about knowing how to fight the disturbing emotions and emerging as a winner.[24]

Use of Weapons

Along with the difficult physical training, using weapons also entails a manly significance for the soldiers. Weapons are an integral part of a particular notion of masculinity that equates "manliness" with the "sanctioned use of aggression, force and violence." Myrttinen (2003) argues that weapons are used as tools to achieve economic and social gains, wielding power over unarmed males and females. He also argues that the public display, the threat of or actual use of weapons, is an intrinsic part of violent, militarized models of masculinity. In the case of Kashmir too, it helps us understand how weapons help sustain masculinity. For instance, a young soldier deployed in Rashtriya Rifles explained:

> This rifle is a part of my body. I don't see it separate from my ownself. I joined the army because of the gun. It makes me feel like a man. When I first went back home after training in the gun, I used to brag about it. People take me more seriously now and they are scared of me. This rifle is my everything. I have turned from a boy to a man.[25]

The Rashtriya Rifles are a force composed of armed forces especially trained for counterinsurgency operations. They undergo rigorous preinduction training and operate in a grid structure to deal with insurgents at high altitudes. Motivational slogans like, "We Train to Win," can be seen on the Rashtriya Rifles training camps. Their motto, as they previously declared on social media platforms, interestingly depicts their perceived sense of power through the name (which translates as "national rifles") of the force:

> Hathiyaar toh shouk se rakhte hain hum Baaki khauf ke liye naam hi kaafi hai
>
> (We hold weapons as a hobby, Our name is enough to create fear.)[26]

The weapons used in the military are usually viewed as extensions of the military body or like the uniform, as an accessory that adds bodily value.

For some soldiers, who were interviewed having a weapon on their body represents both a real and symbolic idealization of aggression and as such functions as an extension of the militarized body. Military weapons and their implicit threat of aggression arguably constitutes the ideals of hegemonic masculinity (Cock, 2001).

The use of weapons to boost manhood is also closely associated with the idea of a crisis of masculinity. As Dolan (2002) argues, conflict situations tend to reinforce narrow views of masculinity whereby the men with weapons have the power and men are often expected to be either warriors and/or protectors by tradition, while failure to live up to these expectations leads to the recourse to weapons. Similarly, Myrttinen (2003) points out that when there is a "fear of loss of male power" due to social transformations, it leads to a backlash in which "traditional" gender roles are more strongly reinforced and weapons "come to support the masculinity under threat." For instance, an army officer posted in Kashmir during the counter insurgency operations of the 1990s, noted this:

> Our guns and rifles are not different from us. They make us powerful. It is the reason that the enemies are scared of us. Yes, without the gun we are nothing, but why do you want to separate the gun from our being? No soldier comes without a gun! Without a gun we will be eunuchs![27]

A significant aspect also pertains to the sexualization of weapons as a way to reinforce masculinity. This can be explained in two ways. On the one hand, it is explained by various feminist scholars that since weapons are seen as extensions of the masculine self, their shape often resembles male body parts. Shape of guns, tanks, cannon, and certain types of aircrafts are important examples. On the other hand, an important metaphor can be seen that visualizes an intimate relationship between the man and weapon. Here, soldiers are taught to feminize tools of war: to view their guns as their bride, as female beings they are expected to take care of. Rashtriya Rifles personnel deployed in Kashmir, are often heard saying, "Duty is my life, and Rifle is my wife." When asked about why they view their rifles as their wives, a soldier said,

> It is like a relationship. Especially when I first got myself trained to use her, it was like that feeling of first love. Now I have to protect her. I feel proud holding her, just as you will with your bride.[28]

It is a common thing for the soldiers to feminize the tools of war. Another young soldier said this:

Yes, we have female names for rifles, tanks, and other tools. It just helps to love our job more. We feel that our lovers are with us and we are protecting them. It makes us feel even more responsible.[29]

A famous picture in a Kargil memorial of a magazine shows a soldier holding a tank labelled by a heart and an Indian actress's name. It says, "from Raveena Tandon to Nawaz Sharif."[30] Women being conflated with military weapons is quintessentially a patriarchal metaphor. Carrying a rifle and imagining it as a lover can be closely associated with pleasure, power, prestige, and responsibility; all are the ideals of masculinity. Further, the sexualization of weapons also points at the gender power relations visible through the intersection of military, masculinity, and sexuality. It further implies women's objectification like rifles to be owned with pride, bringing in a sense of authority and power to the male soldier.

Slogans as Indicators of Contradictions in Masculine Enactments

Slogans in army camps are also significant in the study of masculinities and they tend to question the masculinities of the militants and supporters of militancy. Graffiti, slogans, quotes, and other such materials are an effective medium to understand how a reality is constructed, represented, or understood. These are not neutral representations but "deeply ideological with far reaching consequences on cognition and attitude towards the reality that is represented" (Obeng and Hartford, 2002). For instance, while talking of street art, graffiti and slogans as a mass medium, Lyman Chaffee (1993) explains that these are significant in understanding any given reality because unlike other forms of mass media like electronic and print journalism, they do not aim to be neutral or professional. Their purpose is to advance a cause or an idea. In that sense, these representations are partisan, a nonneutral, politicized medium.

Similarly, McClintock (1987) discusses that street art, graffiti, and slogans are characterized by a direct expression of thought, where the representations are not complex or obscure, rather they are structured to simplify the message, synthesize thoughts and ideas, and project messages and cliches. The research entailed in this book also highlights the significance of such tools as they are crucial contributors to understand the masculine cultural practices evident in the Kashmir conflict. Engravings, slogans, and quotes are present in the army camps, training schools and other areas in Kashmir that are indicative of the creation of hegemonic masculinity by the Indian army. Following are a few examples of such slogans and graffiti:

A slogan written on a state camp that reads, "Get them by their balls, hearts and minds will follow."[31] This slogan points to a few important things. The phrase, "get them by their balls" strongly indicates the use of force or violence is privileged and glorifies aggression against enemies. And more importantly, it fully conforms to the idea of an idealized masculinity where being a man signifies an innate characteristic of showing aggression, use of force and violence. Another important aspect of this phrase is the use of the word "balls," which is essentially directed at the emasculation of the enemy—the insurgents in this case. For, it is through the destruction of the "balls," the enemy shall lose all his manliness and will come under the control of the army. Hence, controlling the masculinity of the enemy is the key to subjugation and subordination, as this will lead to the "hearts and minds" to follow as mentioned in the latter half of the slogan. It is interesting how the message in this slogan is in opposition to the message of Operation Sadhbhawna (goodwill):

Jawan aur Awam, Aman hai Muqaam.[32]
(*The soldier and the people, peace is the destination.*)

The fifteen corps of the Indian army started this operation in 1998 as a "unique humane initiative undertaken by the Indian Army in the Jammu and Kashmir state to address the aspirations of people affected by scrooge of terrorism, sponsored and abetted by Pakistan" (Indian Army website)[33] and runs alongside the ongoing militarized violence. As a contradiction to "get them by their balls, hearts and minds will follow," this operation propagates "winning hearts and minds of the people of Kashmir through compassion and goodwill." As part of this operation, the Indian army officers, since 2010, encouraged their soldiers to learn the local language and customs for reaching out to the public. In the words of an army general, "*Heart is a weapon*," which indicates a contradictory approach toward managing and reaching out to the people. According to Parvez Bukhari (2011), "the army's expanding armoury now includes new weapons like the heart, culture, religion, living standards, quality of life and the sensitivities of the people." And such new tactics have come in response to the changing nature of resistance mobilization in Kashmir that has acquired a new moral dimension over the state forces since 2010. Some billboards and the army website include pictures of the soldiers holding hands of Kashmiri local people and guiding them toward the Haj pilgrimage; soldiers helping local Kashmiri people at the time of floods in 2014.[34] The plan also called for constructing schools, hospitals, and community development projects and included tours for local students to different parts of the country and the improvement of roads and bridges and so on. The tone of messaging of the Indian military on social media platforms keeps changing as well. For instance, the previous aggressive slogans and inciting messages on the Rashtriya Rifles page on Facebook are now (2021) changed to slogans like, "We are there for you: Whenever Asked Where Ever Tasked–Anytime, Any task, Anywhere."[35] The pictures showing military training practices and armory are now changed to army personnel talking to locals and playing with children. Such contradictions in the enactment of military masculinity points towards the fluidity of hegemonic masculine attributes, and perhaps also a potential of transformation. However, the youth in Kashmir mostly don't believe in these imageries and consider them false portrayals. Some locals pointed out:

> What they are doing is a planned strategy for psychological warfare. They want us to believe that they are our caretakers and protectors. How can we ever believe something like that, on the one hand, they have torture camps and on the other hand, they are putting up slogans and pictures of peace.
>
> This drama is to trigger another political unrest so that they can again show their might. They are only psychologically playing games with us to provoke us.
>
> Our struggle is purely a call for political justice, which cannot be achieved within an Indian dispensation. New Delhi is unwilling to negotiate a political solution so this humanistic face of the army is just a way to dress up militarism to deal with further public resistance.[36]

Another important illustration of slogans pertains to the engravings on the Zabarwan hill in Srinagar that reads:

Ajeet hain Abheet hain. ("We are victorious, we are fearless.")[37]

This large slogan engraved on a hill shows a self-conscious attempt to display the idealized masculine characteristics such as victory, bravery, and courage of the Indian army. Two explanations may be offered. This message may be characterized as Chaffee (1993) describes a "territorial demarcation explanation" or it can be understood through the "psychopolitical" and "political intimidation," explanations used for slogans and graffiti. Territorial demarcation explanation is extended to include all the slogans and graffiti that symbolically demarcates a particular area as controlled or liberated, rightly belonging to a specific group or a nation.

Similar slogans are visible such as:

Trespassers will be shot, Survivors will be shot again

POK 600M

BIELARGO 8KM

OLTHING THANG 18KM

SKARDU 129KM

ISLAMABAD WELL WITHIN REACH[38]

Stalkers

Only Best of the Friends and Worst of the Enemies Visit Us Indian Army[39]

These slogans can be read as warning signs for the enemies. Creation of fear and intimidation is another way to prove masculine dominance. A new trend of countergraffiti by the state armed forces also emerged during the protests of 2016. Graffiti became a popular way to express dissent by the Kashmiri youth starting in 2008. "Go India, go back," "We want Freedom," "Inculcate resistance sentiments," and "India, your game is over," are some common examples. The presence of the slogan graffiti increased in the year 2016 which marked an important milestone in the Kashmiri resistance. This was the year when popular young militant-hero Burhan Wani, (belonging to Hizbul Mujahideen militant group) was killed by the Indian security forces. Along with other repressive counterresistance measures, the state armed forces also started overwriting the graffiti of resisters. The countergraffiti painted over words in the existing graffiti, replacing them with new ones to change the meaning of the writing. For instance, "Pak" from "Pak is great" was replaced with India; removing the "go's" and "back" from "Go India, go back," and writing "I love." Similarly, another graffiti, "India, your game is over," was changed to "India, your game is good," and one was overwritten as "I love Modi" (Naqash, 2016).

The battleground is now extended to the words on the roads, camps, and streets. What does this "war of words," which includes state's participation through slogans and countergraffiti really imply? Most simplistically, it high-lights the intent of the state to exert complete control and quell all forms of dissent. In a way, the usefulness of street writing in a political conflict is also acknowledged by the state and it is sometimes hijacked to promote its own political message. The audience to the slogans is the same—Kashmiri inhab-itants of the valley who are largely against the Indian state. The state conveys the message (to the audience) of controlling any form of dissenting expres-sion. The slogans, engravings, and overwriting graffiti is an extension of the challenge and counterchallenge culture in Kashmir conflict, what the locals call—"psychological warfare." Such confrontational sloganeering also, to some extent represents challenges thrown at the others' masculinity—"where one man's defacement is another man's honour" (Amin & Majid, 2018).

The military masculinity of state armed forces entails multiple complexi-ties, contradictions, and nuances. A careful analysis shows that the construct of an idealized masculinity may not always coincide with the lived experiences, practices, or perceptions of men in the military. Sometimes the disciplining and vigorous training practices are used as coping mechanisms by the soldiers to resolve their emotional distress. There are also softer military practices that do not conform to the model of idealized military masculinity. Rather than relying on the existing understanding of hyper masculinity as men's extreme violence, there is a need to rethink the association between men and violence. The study of processes and practices that shape idealized and hegemonic forms of masculinity, puts us in a better position to address different forms of power relations. Unpacking the masculinization process, rather than using it as a reference point for violence, will enable formulation of frameworks that are more engaging and carry the potential for social change. A positive change can be conceptualized if more focus and space is given to a thoughtful analysis of military masculinity that highlights fluidity, interdependence, and contradictions. It is important to go by Duncanson's (2015) suggestion of "shifting from constructing the identity of men in terms of radical othering to forging identities through relations of equality, respect and empathy." Adopting more empathetic approaches to studying men's association with violence, helps in facilitating a more inclusive examination of masculinities. In a similar spirit of reflective assessment of men's identities, the next chapter explores militant masculinities: its intersections with religion and several complexities; and hybridity surrounding the study of masculinities of ex-militants and aspiring militants.

REFERENCES

Amin, Mudasir, and Majid, Iymon. "Politicising the Street: Graffiti in Kashmir." *Economic and Political Weekly*, Vol. 53, Issue 14, 2018.

Anand, Dibyesh. "Anxious Sexualities: Masculinities, Nationalism and Violence." *The British Journal of Politics and International Relations*. Vol. 9, Issue 2, 2007: 257–69. Available at: https://journals.sagepub.com/doi/full/10.1111/j.1467-856x .2007.00282.x.

Batool, Essar, and Rather, Natasha. "The Denial of Rape by Soldiers in Kashmir by the Likes of Shekhar Gupta Illustrates the Impunity Enjoyed by the Armed Forces." *Caravan*. 2016. (Accessed on 09/06/2016). http://www.caravanmagazine .in/vantage/denial-rape-soldiers-kashmir-shekhar-gupta-impunity-armed-forces.

Belkin, Aaron. *Bring Me Men: Military Masculinity and the Benign Façade of American Empire, 1898–2001*, New York: Columbia University Press. 2012.

Bukhari, Parvaiz. "Kashmir: India's Pyramid of Unchanging Policy Posture," *Conveyor*, Vol. 3 Issue 2, April 2011.

Chaffee, Lyman G. *Political Protests and Street Art: Popular Tools for Democratization in Hispanic Countries*, Westport, CT: Greenwood Press. 1993.

Chatterjee, Partha. *The Nation and its Fragments*. Princeton, NJ: Princeton University Press. 1993.

Chengappa, Raj. "Spoils of Holding the Heights." *India Today*, August 6, 1999: 47–50.

Cock, J. "Gun Violence and Masculinity in Contemporary South Africa," in Morrell R. (ed.), *Changing Men in Southern Africa*. Pietermaritzburg, South Africa: University of Natal Press. 2001: 43–55.

Cohn, Carol. "How Can She Claim Equal Rights When She Doesn't Have to Do as Many Push-Ups as I Do? The Framing of Men's Opposition to Women's Equality in the Military." *Men and Masculinities*. Vol. 3, Issue 2, 2000: 131–51.

Dolan, Chris. "Collapsing Masculinities and Weak States: A Case Study of Northern Uganda," in Frances Cleaver (ed.) *Masculinities Matter! Men, Gender and Development*. London: Zed Books. 2002.

Duncanson, Claire. "Hegemonic Macsulinity and the Possibility of Change in Gender Relations." *Men and Masculinities*. Vol. 18, Issue 2, 2015: 231–48.

Elshtain, Jean Bethke. *Women And War*. New York: University of Chicago Press. 1987.

Enloe, Cynthia. *The Curious Feminist: Searching for Women in a New Age of Empire*. Berkeley: University of California Press. 2004.

Ganguly, Sumit, and Fidler, David. P. (eds.). *India and Counter Insurgency: Lessons Learned*. New York: Routledge. 2009.

Goldstein, Joshua S. *War and Gender: How Gender Shapes the War System and Vice Versa*. Cambridge: Cambridge University Press. 2001.

Hansen, Thomas Blom. "Recuperating Masculinity: Hindu Nationalism, Violence and the Exorcism of the Muslim 'Other.'" *Critique of Anthropology*. Vol. 16, Issue 2, 1996: 137–72.

Hooper, Charlotte. *Manly States: Masculinities, International Relations and Gender Politics*, New York: Columbia University Press. 2001.

Kak, Sanjay (ed.) *Witness/Kashmir 1986–2016*. India: Yarabal Press. 2017.

Kasturi, Bhashyam. "The Indian Army's Experience of Counter Insurgency Operations in J & K." *Aakrosh*, April 29, 2012. Available at: http://aakrosh.sasfor.com/aakrosh/the-indian-armys-experience-of-counterinsurgency-operations-in-jk (Accessed on 02/04/2015).

Khalidi, Omar. "Ethnic Group Recruitment in the Indian Army: The Contrasting Cases of Sikhs, Muslims, Gurkhas and Others." *Pacific Affairs*. Vol.74, Issue 4, Winter 2001–2: 529–52.

Khattak, Saba Gul. "Gendered and Violent: Inscribing the Military on the Nation State," in Hussain, Neelam, Mumtaz, S., and Saigol, R. (eds.) *Engendering the Nation State*, Lahore: Simorgh Women's Resource and Publication Centre. 1997.

McClintock, Cynthia. "The Media and Redemocratization in Peru." *Studies in Latin America Popular Culture*. Issue 6. 1987.

Mushtaq, Samreen. "Opinion - The Gendered Face of Violence and Erasure in Kashmir." *E-International Relations*. July 2021. Available at: https://www.e-ir.info/2021/07/06/opinion-the-gendered-face-of-violence-and-erasure-in-kashmir/ (Accessed on: 20/12/21).

Myrittnen, Henri. "Disarming Masculinities" *Women, Men, Peace and Security*, Issue 4. 2003. Available at: ms1.isn.ethz.ch/serviceengine/ . . . /06_Disarming+Masculini ties.pdf (Accessed on: 24/08/2013)

Myrttinen, Henri, Khattab, L., Naujoks, J. "Rethinking Hegemonic Masculinities in Conflict Affected Contexts." *Critical Military Studies*. Vol. 3, Issue 2, 2016: 103–19.

Naqash, Rayan. "Writing on the Wall: In Kashmir Graffiti meets Counter-Graffiti." *Scroll.in.* 2016. Available at: https://scroll.in/magazine/816041/writing-on-the-wall -in-kashmir-graffiti-meets-counter-graffiti (Accessed on 17/12/2020).

Obeng, Samuel Gyasi, and Hartford, Beverly. *Surviving through Obliqueness: Language of Politics in Emerging Democracies*. New York: Nova Science Publishers. 2002.

Pandit, I. "The "Israel Model': The Fragile Paradise of Kashmir Faces an Existential Threat." *Middle East Eye.* December 3, 2019.

Parashar, Swati. "Competing Masculinities, Militarization and the Conflict in Kashmir." *International Feminist Journal of Politics (IFJP)*, Vol. 20, Issue 4, 2018: 663–65.

Peterson, V. Spike. "Gendered Identities, Ideologies and Practices in the Context of War and Militarism," in Laura Sjoberg and Sandra Via (eds.), *Gender, War and Militarism: Feminist Perspectives*. Santa Barbara, CA: Praeger. 2010.

Pettman, Jan Jindy. *Worlding Women: A Feminist International Politics*. New York: Routledge. 1996.

Subramanium, L. N. "CI Operations in Jammu & Kashmir." *Bharat Rakshak Monitor*, Vol. 3, Issue 2. September–October 2000. Also Available at: http://www.bharat -rakshak.com/MONITOR/ISSUE3-2/lns.html (Accessed on 17/03/2013.)

Suman, Maj. Gen. Mrinal. "Women in the Armed Force: Misconceptions and Facts." *Indian Defence Review*, Vol. 25, Issue 1, Jan.–Mar., 2010. Also Available at: http:// www.indiandefencereview.com/interviews/women-in-the-armed-forces/ Accessed on: 21/03/2015.)

Swami, Praveen. "Figures Back Case for Army Rollback in Kashmir." *The Hindu*, October 28, 2011. Also available at: http://www.thehindu.com/news/national/ article2574588.ece (Accessed on 21/03/2012).

Wicks, Stephen. *Warriors and Wildmen: Men, Masculinity, and Gender.* University of Virginia: Bergin & Garvey, 1996.

Young, Iris M. "The Logic of Masculinist Protection: Reflections on the Current Security State." *Journal of Women in Culture and Society.* Vol. 29, Issue.1. 2003:1–25.

"Women Soldiers of Assam Rifles Deployed in Kashmir for Security Operations," Press Trust of India, July 2021. Available at: https://www.ndtv.com/india-news /women-soldiers-of-assam-rifles-deployed-in-kashmir-to-help-in-security -operations-2477212. (Accessed on: 20/12/2021).

NOTES

1.Examples: Andrea Chiovenda, *Crafting Masculine Selves: Culture, War, and Psychodynamics in Afghanistan.* Oxford: Oxford University Press, 2019; Matthew Maycock, *Masculinity and Modern Slavery in Nepal: Transitions into Freedom.* London: Routledge, 2018; Dibyesh Anand, *Hindu Nationalism in India and the Politics of Fear.* London: Palgrave Macmillan, 2011; Farooq Yousaf, *Pakistan, Regional Security and Conflict Resolution: The Pashtun Tribal Areas.* London: Routledge, 2020; Jani De Silva, *Globalization, Terror and Shaming of the Nation: Constructing Local Masculinities in a Sri Lankan Village.* Crewe: Trafford, 2005.

2. Hindutva is a political ideology that advocates an exclusive Hindu nation. The term was first coined by V. D. Savarkar in 1923 in his essay, "Hindutva: Who Is a Hindu?"

3. See, Sjoberg, Laura. *Gender and International Security: Feminist Perspectives.* New York: Taylor and Francis e-library. 2009; and Tickner, J. Ann. *Gendering World Politics.* New York: Columbia University Press. 2001.

4. Quoted from Suman (2010) and similar arguments came up in conversations with retired army officers.

5. Personal interview on 17/10/2013.

6. Personal interview on 29/08/2014.

7. Personal interview, on 21/10/2013.

8. "Rigorous Training of Indian Army" *YouTube*, Available at: https://www.youtube .com/watch?v=G3PRmckS6k4 (Accessed on: 02/10/2014.)

9. Personal interview, as on 12/7/2014 with a commanding officer.

10.Hindu conceptualization of the maternal symbolism is discussed later in chapter 5, where I explore the significance of mother symbols and narratives in reinforcing the militarized masculinities of both the state and non-state actors.

11. As told by a barber in a salon in Delhi, 2015.

12. As told by a group of boys who regularly go to a gym in Gurgaon, 2015.

13. As seen on the notice of recruitment rally in Aantnag, and also available in the general career information on the website of the Indian army.

14. Field marshal Sam Hormusji Framji Jamshedji Manekshaw was the chief of the army staff of the Indian army during the Indo-Pakistan war of 1971 and first Indian army officer to be promoted to the rank of field marshal.

15. Source: Best Proud Indian Army Slogans, Available at: http://bcbilli.com /best-proud-indian-army-slogans-makes-me-proud-to-be-an-indian/ (Accessed on 19/05/2014.)

16. Personal interview, as on 02/05/2013.

17. Mentioned on the Facebook page of Armed Forces Officials Welfare Organization. Available at: https://www.facebook.com/afowosociety/ (Accessed on 14/03/2021.)

18. "Exclusive Report from Corps Battle School, Sarol J&K where Army gets Training to fight Terrorists" *YouTube*. Available at: https://www.youtube.com/watch?v=jz5n4Xdr-tk (Accessed on 14/03/21.)

19. Personal interview, as on 12/7/2014 with a commanding officer.

20. Video showing the training "Soldiers Training in India," available at: https://www.youtube.com/watch?v=AzvDfakP0ek (Accessed on: 20/09/2014.) Also, see "Guerilla Training of Indian Army: Counter Insurgency Training at Corps Battle School, available at: https://www.youtube.com/watch?v=z1w4QVE2SEk (Accessed on 26/11/2018.)

21. Personal interview, 29/08/2014.

22. Personal interview, 29/09/2015.

23. Personal interview, 29/09/2015.

24. Personal interview, 29/09/2015.

25. Personal interview as on 8/29/2014.

26. A number of training practices and slogans of Rashtriya Rifles were earlier available on their Facebook page: https://www.facebook.com/IndianArmyrashtriyaRifles (Accessed on 04/07/2015.)

27. Personal interview as on 5/5/2015 with an army officer posted in Kashmir during 1990s

28. Personal Interview as on 3/9/2014.

29. Personal Interview as on 3/9/2014.

30. Source: *esamskriti.com: The Essence of Indian Culture*, Available at: http://www.esamskriti.com/photo-detail/Kargil-Memorial.aspx (Accessed on 05/06/2014.)

31. A picture of a state camp in South Kashmir in 2008 by Javed Dar in *Conveyor*, Vol. 3 Issue 2, April 2011: 35.

32. More information on Operation Sadhbhavna is available on the Indian army website: https://indianarmy.nic.in/Site/FormTemplete/frmTempSimple.aspx?MnId=HEPwWEmrREvm6FAQs8JeSg==&ParentID=e/J4wC4Y24PIM3XSMyQDWg== (Accessed on 14/03/21.)

33. Ibid.

34. These pictures were seen on the billboards in and around Srinagar. Also, on the Indian army website.

35. The new version of the Indian Rashtriya Rifles page is available here: https://www.facebook.com/rashtriyarifle (Accessed on 14/03/2021.)

36. As told by students in personal interview as on 24/08/2015.

37. *Indian Express*, Mon, 24 June 2013. Available at: http://archive.indianexpress.com/news/omar-objects-army-removes-slogan-from-srinagar-mountain-face/1133001/ (Accessed on 7/7/2014).

38. Preeti Panwar, "Cease Fire Operations, Haven't the Pak Rangers Read 'Islamabad Well Within Reach' Message on the Milestone?" Available at: http://www.oneindia.com/india/haven-t-pak-rangers-read-islamabad-well-within-reach-message-on-milestone-1504095.html (Accessed on 29/ 08/2014).

39. Best Proud Indian Army Slogans, Available at: http://bcbilli.com/best-proud-indian-army-slogans-makes-me-proud-to-be-an-indian/ (Accessed on 19/05/2014).

Chapter 4

Militarized Manhood in the Kashmiri Resistance

The Kashmiri resistance movement provides an example of the coexistence of different forms and complexities of militarized manhood in conflict. The heavy presence of the state military imbued with extraordinary powers, such as the AFSPA, and the resulting human rights violations has resulted in a "vulnerable" (for the lack of a better word) existence for Kashmiri men. Men living under political and economic oppression, experiencing marginalization, feeling dejection, intimidation, and humiliation have seldom any opportunity to prove themselves as "honorable" and/or practice masculinity in culturally prescribed or acceptable ways. Under these circumstances, militant networks have acted as significant outlets to achieve self-actualization, heroism and other idealized characteristics associated with masculinity. In this context, the shaping and creation of militant masculinities is an integral part of the Kashmiri resistance. However, there is not one single model of militant masculinity. The different models of militant masculinity are rooted in the changing political factors and include significant intersections with religion. As discussed in the second chapter, the Kashmiri resistance undertook a Muslim revivalist turn in the 1980s. The refashioning of Islam as a potent weapon for the resistance during this period had a profound impact on the formation of the masculinity of the Mujahid (the warrior-fighter) during the peak of the militancy movement in Kashmir. Later, after the street protests in 2008 and 2010, a new form of indigenous militant masculinities emerged. In this chapter, through the interviews with ex-militants and young boys aspiring to be militants, I will first explore these two different militancy models that provided a platform for men to reassert their sense of manhood. Second, focusing on the narratives of former militants (both ex-militants and surrendered militants), I discuss the demobilized militarized masculinities. In the third part of the chapter, I explore how men associated with various militarized experiences, navigate the gender expectations and exercise their agency.

DIDN'T FEEL MAN ENOUGH TILL I PICKED
UP A GUN: THE MUJAHID OF LATE 1980S

As discussed before, several political factors contributed toward the growing resentment against the Indian state and the party politics in Kashmir in the 1980s. The failure of the National Conference to achieve the promised plebiscite, the signing of the Sheikh-Indira accord, and finally, the rigged elections of 1987 all resulted in discontent and anger among the youth. The absence of an institutional mechanism to address their grievances, further made the youth believe that only an armed resistance could provide the solution. The following narrative of an ex-militant depicts this sentiment of betrayal and inadequacy:

> When I picked up the gun, I did so because I felt cheated by India and the political leaders of Kashmir. When you are cheated you feel like you are stabbed in the back, you feel helpless, you are unable to do anything for your family, your community, you don't feel *man enough*. Most of the boys of our generation felt this sentiment of feeling inadequate, but our religion teaches us to fight against any kind of oppression and that is why the entire community supported us, and I will not deny the fact that the gun brought us back the respect, it brought us back our manhood. (emphasis added)[1]

Inspired by the Iranian revolution, Afghanistan's resistance to Soviet invasion and the Palestinian Intifada, the defense of the Muslim community in Kashmir became the central signifier of the masculinity of the young militant in Kashmir in the late 1980s. The resurgence of the transnational Islam as a political ideology to fight militarism made a significant impact on the Kashmiri resistance movement. The Jamat-e-Islami and other organizations intensified their efforts to circulate Islamic revivalist thoughts and literature to mobilize the youth toward achieving an independent Islamic Kashmir nation. Religion, thus, became a core motivation for young boys to participate in the armed rebellion. Anecdotes suggest that there was an extensive distribution of literature on revolutions based on Islamic liberation ideals (both Shi'a and Sunni), such as a pamphlet titled the "Tragedy of Kashmir." Thousands of copies of Pakistani writer Muhammed Yusuf Saraf's book, *Kashmiris Fight for Freedom* appeared in the valley. The triumph of Ayatollah Khomeini in the Iranian Revolution of 1979 was also used as a source of inspiration, and his talks of Islamic Revolutions around the world to liberate the enslaved Muslim people were used as an instrument to encourage the local Kashmiris to attain freedom. The literature on the success of the Afghans in defeating the Soviet superpower was also used as an important tool to influence the local Kashmiri youth to fight for "freedom." Anecdotes suggest that some literature that had its flourishing grounds from the Afghan refugee camps in Peshawar during Soviet presence in Afghanistan in 1980s were produced at the University of Nebraska–Omaha in late 1980s. Kashmiri youth received these materials in early 1990s.

In the late 1980s and early 1990s, I used to read material on various freedom struggles from around the world such as that of Afghanistan, the material used to come mainly from the University of Nebraska and was distributed to us here by political and religious organizations that supported militancy; the material definitely helped in developing a passion for the movement for freedom and be a hero, a revolutionary.[2]

Non-Islamic revolutionary literature such as *Guerrilla War* by Che Guevara[3] was also widely circulated, which suggests that certain non-Islamic sources of inspirations were also being used to construct the militant masculinity of 1980s. Young boys joined the ISL leaders who formed the armed group Jammu and Kashmir Liberation Front (JKLF) and crossed the line of control to receive arms training in the Pakistan administered Kashmir. Apart from political and religious oppression, economic factors also contributed toward the decision of a few to join the armed rebellion. Some ex-militants mentioned that they joined militancy because of unemployment and poor financial situation.

I didn't have money, I was unemployed, a friend gave me a gun, so I chose to join the movement for freedom rather than sitting idle at home.[4]

The violent resistance and armed struggle provided a crucial pathway toward meeting certain expectations of masculinity that entailed heroic resistance to external oppression (political, religious, and economic) and performing the role of the protector of the Islamic community. This model of Islamic masculinity also draws heavily on local Kashmiri narratives of Azadi (freedom) from the Indian state. The expressions of manhood and heroism in Kashmiri folk songs sung during that time, for instance, point toward the hybridity of the masculinity of the Kashmiri militant. Similarly, cultural practices of decorating the Mujahid as a bridegroom and songs sung by women urging him to get Azadi (freedom) as the bride highlight the importance of the local context in the shaping of militant masculinities.

The day I joined the movement, I was decorated like a groom, with henna on my hands. My mother made me wear garlands. The entire village was singing Kashmiri folk songs of pride and freedom. It was the same story in all villages.[5]

Many Kashmiri Muslims in the valley (both men and women) wholeheartedly supported the militant movement in its initial phases. Young militants were considered heroes and were respected by their community. Women played a significant role in shaping the masculinity of the Mujahid. Young girls, who had entered the marriageable age, desired to marry the militants, whom they viewed as heroes. In social events such as marriages, young women sang couplets praising the militants such as *Kalashnikov lagai balayai yenav ladayat path fairaleh* ("don't give up this fight for freedom, I shower my life on this Kalashnikov"), and *main mujahidov behan paraie hideouts* ("O my beloved militant, I will wait for you at the hideout"). There was competition among women supporters to compose premilitancy couplets (Sobhrajani, 2008). Marrying a militant was a matter of pride in the whole village. Women who married militants said that it was a great honor to marry someone brave enough to take up arms to fight for the cause of Kashmir. In my interviews, two women mentioned that they still kept pictures of the militant-heroes they loved during the armed resistance of the late 1980s.The mothers of militants also earned respect and recognition for sacrificing their sons to the movement. Mothers provided the validation and sanctity to the cause of freedom and encouraged their sons to pick up the guns. The martyrdom of militants was also celebrated and mothers singing songs of glory infused masculinity in the bodies of the dead militants (I will discuss the significance of symbolism and agency of mothers in constructing a militant masculinity in the next chapter). An ex-militant remembered the period of violent resistance of 1980s:

> That was a glory period. All militants were treated with respect as heroes. All boys wanted to pick up the gun and cross the border for training. Picking up arms and fighting for the cause of Azadi gave a sense of purpose. People took pride when any person of their village became a mujahid. It was something all young men in the time of tehriq (movement) aspired to be.[6]

The training experiences of the militants in Pakistan administered Kashmir and exposure to other militant networks shaped their perceptions of manhood. In Husnain's (2000) account of militant training process, and in my own interviews with some ex-militants, the training is described as follows: A new entrant, who had crossed the border first had to undergo a training for three weeks at one of the camps established by the jihadi groups in Muzzafarabad in Pakistan. Here, basic training in handling arms was conducted along with ideological indoctrination. After this initial training was complete, the boys were sent to their respective towns and cities, in Indian-administered Kashmir, where for the next few months they worked as volunteers for different militant groups. The young militants were closely watched and assessed for their commitment to the cause of Jihad. Those selected were sent for a three-month commando training. The teachers at the training centers were former Afghan veterans or senior "Mujahids," who had spent a good part of their lives fighting in the valley. Under their supervision, the boys learned to use AK-47s, handle explosives, and participate in mock attacks on dummy Indian convoys and positions. In all, it costed 1 lakh Indian rupees (approximately 1,400 USD at that time) to train a militant. Their final test was an endurance test. The selected boys had to walk and climb for seventy-two hours without food and water and were allowed a few hours' nap. Once they passed this test, they were ready to cross the border. When asked about the training experience one of the ex-militants responded:

> After a few days of training I felt *the gun to be an extension of me*. We had to go through very difficult training also. We had to climb for days without food or water. It is a miracle how I survived since there were times I felt I was about to die. But I feel that struggle was so pure that even Allah was with us. (emphasis added)[7]

Often ex-militants mentioned witnessing "miracles" in their training practices and in actual combat. Divine protection manifested through miracles became an important proof/justification for their course of actions. The construct of the male warrior/protector in Kashmir has also heavily relied on the use of weapons, mainly guns. Militant groups mobilized the local Kashmiri men into picking up guns. An ex-militant, in an interview, remembered that a militant used to stand at the corner of his house to supply guns to all the young boys; "In our village, at least one man in each household in the 1990s had picked up a gun," and militant leaders implored all local women to sell their jewelery to help finance the purchase of weapons.[8] Crossing the border was also not a simple exercise. There were careful preparations before a militant was sent across the border. According to militants contacted by *Outlook* in the late 1990s, there was a high level of secrecy involved in the entire operation. The militant groups kept a tight lid on the movement and deployment of their cadres in the valley. It was often in the middle of the night that an unmarked vehicle would pick up the two or three militants as per the plan and drop them at one of the designated Pakistani army forward posts along the LOC, depending on the infiltration route. It was at these posts that men in civilian clothes, believed to be ISI officials, handed over an operations kit to each militant. The kit included weapons, ammunition, explosives, and Indian currency. The militants would be given two days to check their weapons and get ready for the final intrusion. Normally, a group would consist of a guide and five to ten militants. Each one carried ten to fifteen kilograms of weapons and stores. Crossing the LOC is seen as the most difficult part of the operation.

Only those who survived the Indian guns and snipers were able to fight in the valley (Outlook, 2000).

According to an ex-militant,

> It took anywhere between three and ten nights for the groups to actually reach the Valley. Once we would cross over, we were guided by the guides to hideouts in the forests. The tactics involved bombings, acts of arson, kidnappings, assassinations, and threats of further violence.[9]

The military training, encounters with both regional and international Islamic militant networks, and actual combat provided the Kashmiri militants a perspective on their own masculinity in relation to other forms of militant masculinities. Also, the encounters with the different militant camps provided an avenue to recalibrate their existing notions of manhood, a new way to be a man, which was tied to the role of defender of the Kashmiri Islamic community.

GUNS, POSES, AND POSTERS: KASHMIR'S NEW FREEDOM FIGHTERS

As the militancy movement of the late 1980s and early 1990s lost popularity among the Kashmiri masses and the human rights violation cases kept rising, the armed militancy had lost all the charm it once possessed. People were disillusioned with the factionalized militant outfits and withdrew their support from violent resistance in the late 1990s (for more, see chapter 2). Some militants also left the movement due to the disunity among the militant groups and realizing that violence cannot bring any solution. The violence of both the state and militant groups had resulted in the loss of many lives and inflicted enormous suffering on the Kashmiri Muslims and Pandits inhabiting the valley. Many militants who surrendered to the state armed forces also stated that the gun culture worsened the situation in Kashmir and caused more suffering among the Kashmiri people. This is echoed in some of the responses of surrendered/ex-militants to whom I asked why they withdrew their support to the armed struggle: "There is no solution with a gun; gun has claimed many precious lives there will be no solution; the solution lies in talks and negotiations between both sides of the Line of Control (LOC) one who holds gun in his hand whether Indian army or militants must know that gun only brings death not peace."[10]

The resentment against the Indian state and politics in Kashmir continued to grow, but the resistance movement was not as strong or violent as before. It was in 2008 that a new street resistance movement spearheaded by the new generation came into existence. Angered by the transfer of land to the Amarnath Shrine Board, Kashmiri youth pelted stones at the state armed forces and their vehicles. A similar street protest also took place in 2010, when a young boy, aged seventeen years, Tufail Mattoo, was killed after being hit in the head with a tear gas shell. He was protesting against state authorities near Gandhi memorial college in Srinagar before he was killed. His death triggered massive protests in the valley and a number of young boys and girls came onto the streets and participated in stone throwing.

What followed was repressive counter techniques by the state armed forces to quell the protests. The Indian state armed forces used shotguns and a large number of resisters suffered pellet injuries; many were blinded. Some of them had pellets in their bodies even while I was conducting interviews with them. They not only suffered physical injuries but because of the recording and profiling carried out by the Central Reserve Police Force (CRPF), they said, they were detained on any public day or were called once in a month for interrogation. A young man who participated in the stone throwing movement stated the following:

> I took the opportunity to take part in the stone pelting because I thought I can express my dissatisfaction without having to leave my home and responsibilities like the militants do. But, now that I see myself and other "stone pelters" being harassed on a regular basis even after the movement is over, I think picking up the gun is definitely a better option where you are either this way or that way.[11]

The constant repression, detentions, and suffering inflicted through pellet injuries can be seen as the roots of the new militant movement in the Kashmir conflict. This new militancy was represented by a "homegrown" Kashmir-based militant outfit, Hizbul Mujahideen, that advocated against the Indian state and suggested a violent insurrection against it. The new-age militants did not cross over to Pakistan for arms training like the first-generation separatist fighters. This new group of militants used social media platforms such as Facebook to post their advocacies and pictures. A picture of a group of militants holding guns and wearing military uniforms became popular. As Masood (2015) and Uzma (2015) argued that unlike the militant of the old times who would never reveal their faces in public, the young Kashmiri militants were brazenly releasing their pictures and videos on social media. A senior counter-insurgency police officer termed this as an attempt to glamorize militancy and attract more youth. Masood (2015) cited a police officer saying that the number of local militants has been steadily rising in the past several years, but in the years 2013–2014, there has been a sudden increase. In this context, Handoo (2015) writes about the link between the unabated harassment faced by youth having a stone-pelting history, which served as a tipping point in the emergence of the new militant movement.

The leader of the new militancy, Burhan Wani, became the popular poster boy in Kashmir. In July of 2016, at the age of twenty-two, he was killed by the Indian security forces, but before his death, his online images as a freedom fighter created the desire among the young men in Kashmir to fight. This young, delicate, good-looking, middle-class boy-next-door-turned-militant became an inspiration and brought a renewed sense of manhood among young boys in Kashmir.[12] Pictures of Burhan wearing a militant uniform, a green bandana with Quranic inscriptions, and holding a gun were widely circulated on the internet. The walls of the villages in south Kashmir started bearing graffiti of Burhan's militancy and heroism from 2013 onwards. Messages like "Burhan's Recruiting," "Burhan—the pride of Kashmir," were highly visible. Many young boys in the interviews during 2014 and 2015 mentioned that they aspired to be like Burhan and if they had a chance, they would join his militant group as they felt harassed with the detentions and regular interrogations. Burhan became a potent symbol of the new armed resistance due to this glamorized, modern Kashmiri militant imagery, with its relatability with the Kashmiri youth. Along with its appeal, the circulation of Burhan's presence on social media and graffiti also coincided with the growing resentment among the young resisters against the repressive state measures. In my interviews with the young participants of the stone-pelting movement of 2008 and 2010, they clearly pointed out that through Burhan's new militancy movement, they found a hopeful avenue to express their anger and discontent against the Indian state.

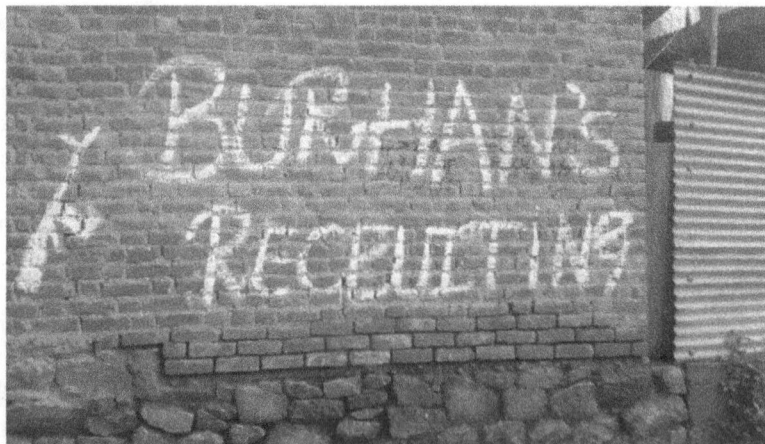

Figure 4.1 Message on the wall of a village in South Kashmir, Photo: Amya Agarwal

Figure 4.2 Another graffiti in a village in South Kashmir, Photo: Amya Agarwal

With the emergence of the new militancy in Kashmir, a new trend started where young, highly educated, middle-class men left their jobs to join the armed resistance. Some were civil engineers, sons of doctors, and so on. Tral, from which Burhan Wani and some other new generation militants hailed, has the highest literacy rates in Kashmir. Some studies and narratives had earlier suggested that unemployment and lack of education were the main reasons for young men joining militancy in the 1980s.[13] In the new militancy, education and employment of militants is thus a highlighted aspect in my interviews with local people and media reporting (Ahmed, 2018). A student who participated in the stone-throwing movement pointed out that "when the militant movement started in the late 1980s, many people thought that the men who joined the movement were unemployed and uneducated, so they joined it. But now educated youth have started participating in the movement to prove that correlation [between unemployment, lack of education and joining the militancy] wrong."[14]

In addition to the educated and middle-class backgrounds, the new model of militant masculinity draws on Islamic motivations. However, it is not as transnational as the earlier militancy was. This maybe because exposure of the new generation of militants is limited to the Kashmiri region as opposed to the earlier encounters with international militant networks. However,

iconographies drawing on the Quran, Islamic flags, green headbands suggest the religious inflections are still strongly present in the space of the
new militancy. There is also a strong presence of the "modern" in this new
militant masculinity model represented through the presence of smartphones,
sport-watches along with Kalashnikovs in the images; and does not include
certain elements usually associated with extremists, such as long beards and
traditional kohl (Hartwell, 2017). The militants of the present sport shorter
beards depicting a sort of hybrid (of both Islamic and non-Islamic) revolutionary persona. It draws more on the modern version of Kashmiri Muslim
civilian manhood that regards education, employment and an economic status
as important pathways to manhood and also incorporates the ultra-conserva-
tive Sunni religious aspects of the region.

The new militancy received huge support from Kashmiri Muslim men and
women. The bravery and courage of the group to take up arms and publicly
announce their violent resistance against the Indian state was applauded by
the local Kashmiris, especially the youth (Bukhari, 2016; Gowen, 2016).
Some mothers of sons killed during the protests of 2010 and those who suffered pellet injuries, gave their whole-hearted support and encouragement to
the new militancy movement. The support continued even after Wani's death.
The martyrdom of Wani was celebrated by a large gathering of Kashmiris
in the valley. Several pictures and videos from Wani's funeral circulated on
the internet that suggest the massive support he received from the Kashmiri
Muslim masses. His death also triggered enormous civil unrest. Street protests by young students in different areas in Kashmir along with various
forms of resistance by young men and women became more frequent in 2016
in the Kashmir valley. In response, along with the violent counterprotests
techniques, the state cut the internet to prevent organization of resistance
through social media.

Wani's militancy also throws light at the multiple ways in which militant
male bodies are deployed (both alive or dead) in resistance and conflict. How
militant bodies are deployed is also closely associated with the notions of
masculinity. Jani De Silva (2014), in her study of militant masculinities in
Sri Lanka, for instance, explores the significance of the body in reinforcing
masculinities. She argues that "attributes such as violence, valor, aggression,
confidence, composure and deference are inscribed upon the body and its
demeanors." Similarly, in the case of Kashmir, masculine attributes of bravery, valor, confidence, and honor are infused in the live and dead militant
bodies. Right from Wani's body portrayal as the brave yet delicate, modern,
glamorous and religious militant through his social media presence; and later
to the pictures and posters of his martyrdom serve the different purposes of
the resistance movement. Posters with his pictures saying "Pride of Kashmir"
and "Burhan is still alive" were visible not only in the valley after his death

but are also highly visible on the internet. This hyper-visibility of martyrs, like Wani, points toward harnessing their service to the broad resistance and militant projects. Myrttinen (2020) articulates this hyper-visibility succinctly in his study of the iconography of Lebanese martyrs:

> The martyrs' photos fit into broader established narratives of both secular and more religious informed (both Christians and Muslims) sacrifice, heroism, self-lessness—and a call for others to follow their sacrificial example.

On the other hand, however, the pictures of dead militant bodies also serve Indian nationalist and othering purposes of the state military. For instance, Wani's dead face and messages of him asking for forgiveness, disseminated on WhatsApp helped in the construction of the victory over the "Muslim ter-rorist" enemy narrative. The popularity of the dead militant was also utilized effectively by the Indian army to prove its own might and strength (Hartwell, 2017). Furthermore, the Arab masculinity depicted in Western discourses as Amar (2011) critiques them: "atavistic, misogynist and hypersexual mascu-linities" enables the easy othering of the Kashmiri Muslim masculinity as "criminal terrorists."

An interesting reinstatement of Wani's masculinity after his death was vis-ible through his techno-masculinization in the video game "Burhan vs Modi." This game was developed for Android phones and was downloaded and shared through file sharing applications such as "Share It" in Kashmir (Saha, 2016). In the game, the goal is to reach Azadi (freedom) and the character "dons Wani's character and shoots, kicks and punches to eliminate Modi-like character to gain points" (Saha, 2016). Such platforms are significant avenues to not only remasculinize the living militants, but they also embody superhu-man masculinity in the dead male bodies of the martyrs. More than viewing these acts as neoliberal assertions of militarized masculinity, these can be viewed as "beyond the grave" agency of the dead militants.

DEMOBILIZED MILITARIZED MASCULINITIES OF EX/SURRENDERED MILITANTS

The United Nations Department of Peacekeeping Operations (UNDPO) defines the terms "demobilization" and "reintegration" (as part of the disarma-ment, demobilization, and reintegration [DDR] programs for ex-combatants) as follows: "demobilization involves the concentration, quartering, disarm-ing, management and licensing of former combatants who may receive some form of compensation or other assistance to motivate them to lay down their weapons and re-enter civilian life" and "reintegration or reinsertion consists of those measures directed toward ex-combatants that seek to strengthen the capacity of these individuals and their families to achieve social and economic reintegration in society."[15]

In concurrence with the above definitions, several efforts have been made by the Indian state and international NGOs to demobilize and reintegrate the former militants in the civilian life of the Kashmir valley. The Indian state (both at the center and state level) implemented the "Surrender and Rehabilitation Policies" in 1995, with subsequent revisions in 2004, 2010, and 2019. These policies have aimed to "motivate militants to surrender and to re-integrate them in the Kashmiri society" (Bhayana, 2019). They provide former militants compensation, vocational training, and employment at the Ikhwan force (a pro-government militia), while some surrendered militants are also absorbed in paramilitary forces and territorial army, along with receiving cash and stipend. The focus of this policy is mainly monetary benefits, and the primary motive is to bring back the militants from Pakistan administered Kashmir, "as there remains a danger of Pakistan using them as strategic reserves against India in future" (Bhayana, 2019). The policy, however, does not consider the social challenges that these men go through during the reintegration process. In this section, I discuss how little access the former militants have to civilian symbols of masculine prestige. This discussion is based on the interviews with the ex/surrendered militants who had joined the militancy movement in the late 1980s.

In the sociological context of Kashmir, especially in terms of honor and disgrace, there is a distinction between the terms "ex-militant" and "surrendered militant." Surrendered militants are considered to be a more disgraceful category in the Kashmiri nationalist discourse than the ex-militants because the former are supposed to have switched sides and helped security forces as informers/fighters so they are considered to have ostensibly "betrayed the cause." The ex-militants gave up the path of violence but may still be wedded to the Kashmiri cause and, hence, they are relatively better off in the society. Together, however, for analytical purposes, they represent demobilized militarized masculinities. As opposed to the overwhelming support the militants received during the peak of the militancy movement, they were not as respected once they returned to civilian life. The lack of overall support to the militancy in the 1990s due to the inability to achieve independence, along with an increased violence of the Indian state armed forces, and the disunity among the armed groups changed the social position of militancy in Kashmir. The return of militants to the civilian life during this period of distrust toward militancy made their reintegration more challenging.

The challenges of former militants returning to civilian life in Kashmir are somewhat similar to other armed conflict contexts. Some of the surrendered militants I interviewed felt unwelcomed by the society and felt being treated as subordinate citizens. Some felt that they were accepted only by their families. Being labelled as a former militant, they mentioned, "raised suspicion among the people and were considered guilty."[16] Relatively younger ex-militants had insecurities related to marriage and starting a family. This was a complete reversal to their societal position at the time of joining militancy. The label of being ex-militants also affected the lives of their children. Few of them said that their children were unable to pursue education in good schools and colleges due to the militant past of their fathers. For instance, Sadunullah Malik (name changed) mentioned this:

> My children feel that I have completely spoiled their future, they are labelled as children of ex-militants due to which they have trouble getting admissions in colleges. I myself feel guilty. My family taunts me and blames me for my past.[17]

Apart from the above social alienation, the self-investment of the former militants to militarize themselves results in what Theidon (2009) calls "bodily capital" and this becomes an obstacle during the transition to civilian life. As she explains in her study of Colombian ex-combatants, that the "high premium placed on the physical force and prowess with a weapon" and the goals of achieving social mobility when the ex-combatants joined armed groups, does not help much in the civilian labor market. Similarly, performativity of social interactions and limiting the range of emotions are an integral part of militarization—such learned behavior makes the transition even more challenging. In Kashmir too, the body posturing and disciplining of emotions that is learnt during the militarization period, makes others suspicious toward them when they return to civilian life. Also, the fantasy of reunion with family often contrasts with the reality of domestic issues. This sometimes also results in domestic violence. The narrative of Nazim Sheikh (name changed) highlights domestic problems arising during the reintegration of the former militants:

> I am unable to work anymore due to the torture I went through. Life has become worse for me after I returned. My wife used to quarrel with me not only because I could not work but because I had changed. But the circumstances now don't allow me to be the same. I cannot believe that it is the same people of my village who had encouraged me when I picked up the gun, now look down upon me. It is the same circumstances at home that compelled me to give my wife a divorce and now she has remarried. My brother-in-law takes financial care of me, my son and my old mother. Now I am living for my son to grow up and after that I will wait for Allah to take me.[18]

The "struggle masculinity" (or "frustration aggression" [Porter 2013]) of ex-combatants as Xaba (2010) describes in his study of black South African youth who were associated with the antiapartheid struggle were endowed with respect and status as "young lions" and "liberators" within their communities, and their violence was revered. However, the struggle version of masculinity is no longer acceptable in the post-apartheid order and, hence, they faced a crisis of masculinity. As a result, the reassertion of masculinity at home results in increased episodes of domestic violence. Such analyses are not to justify their violent behavior at home, but to understand the different manifestations of masculine violence. The reintegration processes seldom accounts for such complexities of social performativity, emotions, and sentiments, which leaves the former militants to navigate their alienation with little outside support. The alienation of the former militants also includes enormous economic insecurities due to lack of skills and sometimes education. Some former militants after their return felt unable to attain the means of livelihood. Despite the surrender and rehabilitation policy of the state, they couldn't make the ends meet. Two respondents had the following experiences:

> I had crossed the border when I was very young and I have no skills to get a job, neither am I educated. I cannot earn and provide for my family. My wife started working when I was away and she continues to do so.[19]
>
> Even to return, I had to spend my own money as I took an illegal route via Nepal and Uttar Pradesh, because in Pakistan we are not allowed to return back officially. Most of us don't even have a Pakistani passport and had to come back with the support of illegal documents. I don't think it was such a good idea to return because my financial problem has not improved.[20]

For many of the interviewed surrendered militants, the monetary benefits offered in the surrender and rehabilitation policy had attracted them to return. However, the compensation they received did not cover their return journey and was inadequate to sustain their lives; many also said that it came at a high cost—detentions, social rejection, and subordination.

In addition to the social, economic and identity crises, the past experiences of physical and, sometimes, sexual violence also heightened the feelings of inadequacy among some former militants. The interviewees were quite vocal about the physical torture they endured during their detention and arrests. They showed the marks of injuries on their arms, legs, and hands. Some survivors of physical violence mentioned that they were unable to work and were confined to their homes. "My legs are weak, and I am unable to carry out any work, so I stay at home."[21] Few wives of survivors of physical violence also mentioned they had to assume (or continue to assume) the role of the breadwinner because their husbands are unable to work due to the physical violence they endured. For example, Raha B (name changed), like other women whose husband was picked up by the Indian state security forces, had to take over the bread-earning responsibility along with household chores and childcare responsibilities. Although Raha B's husband returned, but he was unable to physically work due to long physical torture. She not only became the earning member of the family, but later also assumed the responsibility of an elected representative of the Panchayat Halqa in her village. Her son mentioned:

> I look up to my mother as my father. Whatever important decisions I have taken in life have been taken by her. My father has gone through a lot and it's not possible for him to take care of us. He is physically weak due to repetitive torture, my mother gives him money to incur daily expenses of household, he takes care of smaller things of the house.[22]

While vocal about the endurance of violence by the state armed forces, some former militants assumed long silences when narrating their victimhood—they were not so comfortable in sharing some of their humiliating experiences during the torture. Out of all the interviewed survivors of physical violence, three former militants confirmed their experiences of sexual violence (not anal rape, but mostly genital trauma). Along with confirming their experiences of what they called "extreme torture," one of them remarked:

> More vulgar forms of torture take place in the torture cells, but I don't want to share more details. All I can say is that the torture is so ugly that can't be described in words.

Contrary to the research findings in other armed conflict areas around the world (as discussed briefly in chapter 2), there is not much research on sexual violence against men in Kashmir, let alone formation of help-groups of survivors of sexual violence. Most survivors prefer to remain silent, however, through very few of my own interviews and a few documented and published cases by human rights organizations such as JKCCS, there is evidence to suggest the existence of sexual violence. For instance, Wani Malik, taken by the Border Security Force personnel in 2005, narrated:

> they sprinkled petrol on my private parts, thrashed me ruthlessly, pulled up hair of my beard with pliers, gave electric shocks on my genitals and finally threw a burning cigarette on my penis. They even injected petrol on my anus. I cried for help but they kept laughing.[23]

A popular sexologist in Kashmir also mentioned that men came to his clinic due to the inability to procreate as a result of genital injuries and high stress levels.[24] However, such discussions are not explicit in the valley, which could be due to the conservative nature of the Kashmiri society along with the deliberate silence of the survivors of sexual violence. It is, therefore, difficult to get the precise and detailed data, apart from the fact that it (may have or continues to) happens. It is important to note here that the sexual violence experiences that men mentioned were different from anal rape. In other words, they did not mention anal rape, but some talked about the existence of other forms (which are also documented in NGO reports) such as forced nudity, castration, penile amputation, genital violence, and sexual humiliation, which are all included as sexual violence (Ba and Bhopal, 2017; Chynoweth et al., 2020, Touquet et al., 2021).

At a first glance, the narratives of former militants on physical and sexual violence, strongly resonate with the "feminization" and "emasculation" narrative; because these men felt ashamed, humiliated, and inadequate at social and economic levels, along the lines of "not feeling like a man." However, the simplistic use of these terms to denote the overall situation of men (both militants and civilians) in the conflict-affected Kashmiri society, and the impulse to render Kashmiri valley and the men as emasculated needs to be addressed more deeply. In a similar light, on rereading the transcripts and interviews, I felt there is a need to go beyond essentializing the vulnerabilities of male survivors of physical and sexual violence as loss of manhood. That is because there is more beyond such projection. In unsaid and often unconscious ways, the militarized men navigate their vulnerabilities and lived realities to make sense of their lives. I elaborate more on this in the next section where I explore the agency of militarized men in navigating their vulnerabilities and their experiences of militarized violence.

INTERWOVEN AGENCY AND VULNERABILITIES OF MILITARIZED MEN

The masculine expectations of Kashmiri society on demobilized militarized men (and also civilian men) sometimes result in the creation of male vulnerabilities and insecurities. However, men exercise their agency while navigating through their militant past and present challenges of reintegration. Surviving both physical (and/or sexual) violence may have categorized the survivors as "victims"; however, they simultaneously navigate their vulnerabilities. My respondents (ex-combatants) who had been arrested, detained, or had surrendered to the Indian state armed forces, showed the injury marks on their bodies. They mentioned that they received these during "torture" at the army camps. They described various torture techniques used by the Indian army, which entailed infliction of extreme harm mostly physically but sometimes sexually (not rape, but genital injuries). The injury marks on the legs, back, shoulder, and hands seemed like combined badges of victimhood and masculinity. Surviving the violence that they described, was, on the one hand, perceived as quite heroic, and on the other hand, evidently rendered them as victims.

Furthermore, the use of the word "torture" is quite common in the valley. Men and women often described the violence (mostly physical and sometimes sexual) endured by a survivor as "torture." Interrogations following detentions, included torture of former militants or suspected civilians in the form of beatings and extreme forms of harm. The frequent usage of "torture" as a household term for the physical violence, in some ways, provided the courage to the survivors to voice out and narrate their oppressive experiences. As victims of torture, the demobilized militarized men are also able to claim a significant space in the Kashmiri society and engage with human rights organizations and civil society bodies. Unlike other contexts, there are not many survivor groups in Kashmir that address the concerns of former militants or survivors of torture, however, the informal ways in which they share experiences among themselves and others have become their significant coping mechanisms.

Performing the role of a family provider is a significant expectation for men in Kashmir. After their return, however, some of the interviewed former militants could not perform this role mainly due to the lack of job skills and/ or physical injuries as discussed before. They felt inadequate due to their inabilities; however, not all of them felt like they were less of a man. Few of them, in fact, embraced their limitations and inabilities to perform the expected masculine roles. As the gender roles at home were reconfigured, women took up the role of the breadwinner, but some of the men did not find it a threat to their masculinity. Some stayed at home, some went to meet their friends and relatives, and some took care of the household chores and children. For example, a former militant, Mahib (name changed) said this:

> When I was taken by the security forces, it was my wife who took over all my responsibilities, she used to do farming, take care of children and the house. She knows everything and takes all important decisions for the house. I don't feel ashamed to sit at home.[25]

The inability to perform the traditional masculine roles did not create insecurity for men like Mahib. To some extent, his violent militant past also provided the cover of masculinity in the present; in other words, his current masculine role and status was not questioned by others. Despite former militants' feelings of societal rejection and labelling, the local people in Kashmir had largely accepted their return and acknowledged their changed position in civilian life. Most of these former militants had friends or relatives who had gone through a similar experience and often got together at each other's houses to talk. They could relate to each other and often shared their problems regarding their return to civilian life. The feelings of humiliation, shame, and vulnerabilities existed; however, these were equally felt by all men in Kashmir—whether militarized or not—and did not necessarily have an impact on their (former militants') perception of manhood. In fact, their exchange of past experiences and stories of oppression enabled the political mobilization of the youth, who saw their wounds of physical "torture" and listened to their stories.

The agency of the former militants, however, is not limited to their articulation of violent experiences and engagement with civil society. Sometimes, they also practice deliberate (not imposed) silence on issues that heighten their feelings of inadequacy. This was particularly evident when few of them chose to remain silent on subjects related to sexual violence, or, regarding the extreme humiliation they suffered during interrogation, or, also when asked about the problems encountered during their time in militancy. Silence, as some scholars, have pointed out, is as important as voice in understanding agency in conflicts. For instance, Mannergren-Selimovic (2020) puts it rightly:

> Silence can be employed for subordination and erasure, but can also be a strategy for coping with a precarious everyday, a form of tacit communication of ambiguity as well as a claim-making strategy.

Similarly, Parpart and Parashar (2020) through their respective studies show how chosen silence can be a powerful form of agency; and in a similar light they criticize the symbolism of silence as powerlessness and passivity. Similarly, in Touquet and Schulz (2020), Schulz through his case study of a male survivor of sexual violence, Okidi in Uganda and Touquet through the case of T, a Croatian survivor, show how male survivors "choose which stories to narrate in which spheres and where to maintain what could be referred as 'protective silence.'" The strategic navigation between protective silence and conscious disclosure of their victimhood challenges the over simplification of agency as moving beyond the silence of victimhood.

As compared to some other conflict-affected contexts, there are fewer programs aimed specifically at survivors of torture in Kashmir. Considering it is a highly militarized zone with instances of enforced disappearances, detentions, and arrests, specific spaces for assistance in the case of torture are almost negligible. Although, alongside militarization, Kashmir has a presence of NGOs, both Kashmiri and international, that provides some (though limited) general space to the survivors of violence to engage. The former militants and civilian men are, however, wary of the available spaces and use discretion in their engagement with civil society bodies. One former militant mentioned that he doesn't give interviews or engages much with outside NGOs to discuss his problems. He said this:

> In Kashmir, now the situation is that one cannot trust anyone. People who were supporters of militancy in the past, have now become informers of the police and state armed forces. Also, there is huge surveillance in the valley. One must give a serious thought to giving what information to whom. For my own concerns and problems, I only go to local organizations whom I am sure of. I don't trust any outside NGO or organization.[26]

"Giving what information to whom" is also a significant form of agency exercised by the male survivors of torture in Kashmir. Trust is an important consideration in the exercise of the agency because of the severely fragmented nature of Kashmiri civilian society in terms of the loyalties. The "loyalty" aspect was touched upon by many interviewees belonging to different vantage points. Some mentioned that it is hard to tell who is associated to which militarized camp and that's why using discretion and silence in narrating their past experiences of violence, or giving opinions regarding the oppression, is considered important by many former militants. Beyond the discretionary engagement with the nonstate actors, however, they do have their close-knit, trusted circles in the form of close friends and male relatives where they go for advice, discuss the political situation, and find a solution to their problems. The coping strategies are mostly informal and unstructured as compared to other contexts where structural harm-responsive mechanisms are accessible to survivors of torture.

It is also important to mention here that the younger generation that was involved in the stone-throwing movements in the past and were subsequently detained, interrogated, and suffered pellet injuries have developed different coping strategies and choices to exercise agency, and are more vocal than men of older generations. Also, their activism shows the intersections between victimhood and agency. Many young resisters (after and during the protests) opted for creative methods of resistance, such as poetry, art, and music. They extensively used the internet not only to share their creative endeavors but also to communicate with communities and people who had resonating experiences. For instance, through social media platforms, Kashmiris and their Palestinian counterparts exchange experiences, express solidarity, and narrate their victimhood. A fascinating exchange of resistance ideas between the Kashmiri and Palestinian activists was seen on Facebook: a Kashmiri newspaper reported how the street protestors in Kashmir had learned to manufacture protection made out of X-ray films as a contraption against the pellets from Palestinian activists on Facebook (Bazaz, 2016). Apart from Palestinian forums on Facebook, the solidarity and informal collaboration can also be seen in blogs like *Palestine for Kashmir*.[27] The blog translates Kashmiri news, reports, resistance poetry, and other writings in Arabic. *Electronic Intifada* is another such platform where Palestinians express solidarity with the Kashmiri resistance.[28] Kashmiri and Palestinian intellectuals also pen down their individual and collective resistance through academic blogs. Various forums, conversational, and collective writings have also become a significant expression of resistance and are easily available on the internet. Although, the Indian state cut the internet connectivity of the valley for six months during the protests of 2016,[29] however, the choice of exercising agency through virtual platforms also confirms the use of victimhood as a powerful category for political mobilization and gaining international solidarity. This simultaneous navigation through victimhood, vulnerabilities, and activism by the resisters in Kashmir, questions the linearity in the existing predominant conceptualization of victimhood and agency.

The militants of the 1980s armed resistance, aspiring militants of the new militancy movement, and demobilized militarized men all show the coexistence, intersection, and overlap of multiple masculinities. Alongside, the discussions on the demobilized masculinities of the former militants suggest that we must move beyond framing their experiences as lost masculinity and instead shift our analysis to their agency in navigating their perceived vulnerabilities. There are multiple ways in which men address their victimhood and make choices that are shaped by the sociopolitical contexts and available spaces of engagement. Voice, silence, discretionary disclosure, and selective engagement are employed by the former militants as significant coping strategies. In Kashmir, unstructured and informal ways of coping are more accessible for the survivors of torture due to the relative absence of structured mechanisms. In the same context, it is also significant to view victimhood and agency of male survivors as an interwoven phenomenon. These are not separate binaries and deserve to be studied with more care because it involves the risk of categorising male victims as passive and incapable, devoid of any agency. The discussions also show how in the contemporary resistance movement (2008 onwards) victimhood has emerged as a powerful category of mobilization and solidarity, which highlights the dynamic between victimhood and agency.

REFERENCES

Ahmed, Mudasir. "Why Educated Kashmiri Youth Continue to Join Militancy." *The Wire*, October, 2018. Available at: https://thewire.in/politics/why-educated -kashmiri-youth-continue-to-join-militancy (Accessed on 04/06/2021).

Amar, Paul. "Middle East Masculinity Studies Discourses of 'Men in Crisis': Industries of Gender in Revolution." *Journal of Middle East Women's Studies*. Vol. 7, Issue 3, 2011: 36–70.

Ba, I., and Bhopal, R. S. "Physical, Mental and Social Consequences in Civilians Who Have Experienced War-Related Sexual Violence: A Systematic Review (1981–2014)." *Public Health*, Vol. 142, 2017: 121–35.

Bazaz, P. N. *The History of Struggle for Freedom in Kashmir*. Srinagar: Gulshan Books, 1954.

Behera, Navnita C. *State, Identity & Violence: Jammu, Kashmir, and Ladakh*. New Delhi: Manohar Publishers and Distributors, 2000.

Bhayana, Arshiya. "Reintegrating Kashmir's Ex-Militants: An Examination of India's Surrender and Rehabilitation Policy." *ORF Issue Brief*. October, 2019. Available at: https://www.orfonline.org/research/reintegrating-kashmirs-ex-militants-an-examination-of-indias-surrender-and-rehabilitation-policy-56044/ (Accessed on 31/03/2021).

Bukhari, Shujaat. "Why the Death of Militant Burhan Wani Has Kashmiris Up in Arms?" *BBC India*, 2016. Available at: https://www.bbc.com/news/world-asia-india-36762043 (Accessed on 26/06/2021).

Chynoweth, S. K., Buscher, D., Martin, S., and Zwi, A. B. "Characteristics and Impacts of Sexual Violence against Men and Boys in Conflict and Displacement: A Multicountry Exploratory Study." *Journal of Interpersonal Violence*. 2020: 1–32.

"Crossing Line: Operation Owl," in *Outlook*, 25 September 2000.

Gowen, Annie. "This Violent Militant was a Folk Hero on Social Media: Now his death has roiled Indian Kashmir." *The Washington Post*. July 2016. Available at: https://www.washingtonpost.com/news/worldviews/wp/2016/07/11/this-violent-militant-was-a-folk-hero-on-social-media-now-his-death-has-roiled-indian-kashmir/ (Accessed on 26/06/2021).

Handoo, Bilal. "Rebel Resurrection?" Available at *kashmirlife.net*. (Accessed on 07/08/2015.)

Hartwell, Fabian. "Burhan Wani and the Masculinities of the Indian State." *Journal of Extreme Anthropology*. Vol.1, Issue 3, 2017: 125–38.

Husnain, Ghulam. "Ready For Jehad: First Hand Account from Pakistan on How the Proxy War Is Bred and Sustained." *Outlook*. September 25, 2000.

Mannergren-Selimovic, Johanna. "Gendered Silences in a Post-Conflict Societies: A Typology." *Peacebuilding*, Vol. 8, Issue 1, 2020: 1–15.

Masood, Bashaarat. "Guns and Poses: The New Crop of Militants in Kashmir." *Indian Express*. July 26, 2015.

Myrttinen, Henri. "Death Becomes Him. The Hyper-Visibility of Martyrdom and Invisibility of the Wounded in the Iconography of Lebanese Militarised Masculinities," in Baker, Catherine (ed.) *Making War on Bodies: Militarisation, Aesthetics and Embodiment in International Politics*. Edinburgh, UK: Edinburgh University Press, 2020.

Parpart, Jane L., and Parashar, Swati (eds.). *Rethinking Silence, Voice and Agency in Contested Gendered Terrains*. New York: Routledge, 2020.

Porter, A. "What is Constructed Can Be Transformed: Masculinities in Post-Conflict Societies in Africa." *International Peacekeeping*. Vol. 20, Issue 4, 2013: 486–506.

Saha, Abhishek. "'Burhan vs Modi': Video game in Kashmir Shows Wani fighting for 'Freedom.'" *Hindustan Times*, November 2016. Available at: https://www.hindustantimes.com/india-news/burhan-vs-modi-video-game-in-kashmir-shows-wani-fighting-for-freedom/story-bi2SzXhM2SsPj8PDiBDsRN.html (Accessed on 31/03/2021).

Silva, Jani de. "Valour, Violence and the Ethics of Struggle: Constructing Militant Masculinities in Sri Lanka." *South Asian History and Culture*. Vol. 5, Issue 4, 2014: 438–536.

Sjoberg, Laura, and Gentry, C. *Mothers, Monsters, Whores: Women's Violence in Global Politics*. London and New York: Zed Books, 2007.

Sobhrajani, Manisha. "Women's Role in the Post-1989 Insurgency." *Faultlines*. Vol. 19, Issue 3, April 2008. Available At: http://www.satp.org/satporgtp/pulication/faultlines/Volume19/Article3.htm (Accessed on 02/04/2013).

Theidon, Kimberly. "Reconstructing Masculinities: The Disarmament, Demobilization and the Reintegration of Former Combatants in Colombia." *Human Rights Quarterly*. Vol. 31, 2009: 1–34.

Touquet, H., Chynoweth, S., Martin, S., Reis, C., Myrttinen, H., Schulz, P., Turner, L., and Duriesmith, D. "From "It Rarely Happens to 'It's Worse for Men': Dispelling Misconceptions About Sexual Violence against Men and Boys in Conflict and Displacement." *Journal of Humanitarian Affairs*. Vol. 2, Issue. 3, 2021. Available at: https://www.manchesteropenhive.com/view/journals/jha/2/3/article-p25.xml (Accessed on 25/03/21).

Touquet, H., and Schulz, P. "Navigating Vulnerabilities and Masculinities: How Gendered Contexts Shape the Agency of Male Sexual Violence Survivors." *Security Dialogue*. 2020: 1–18.

Uzma, Falak. "Kashmir's Wave of Quality Militancy." *New Internationalist Blog*. Available at: http://newint. Org/blog/2015/08/11/Kashmir-armed-youth-challenge-india/ (Accessed on 12/08/2015.)

Xaba, Thokozani. "Masculinity and its Malcontents: The Confrontation between 'Struggle Masculinity' and 'Post-Struggle Masculinity' (1990–1997)," in Robert Morell (ed.), *Changing Men in Southern Africa*. London: Zed Books, 2010.

NOTES

1. Personal interview on 28/08/2014.
2. Personal interview on 1/09/2014.
3. K. N. Pandita, "Kashmir Question," in *Kashmir Herald*. Vol. 2, No. 9, February 2003.
4. Personal interview on 29/08/2014.
5. Personal interview on 22/06/2013.
6. Personal interview on 18/08/2014.
7. Personal interview on 28/08/2014.

8. Personal interview on 28/08/2014.

9. Personal interview on 14/08/2015.

10. Personal interview on 21/07/2014.

11. Personal interview on 29/07/2015.

12. As indicated in interviews with young boys.

13. For example, see Navnita C. Behera, *State, Identity & Violence: Jammu, Kashmir, and Ladakh*, New Delhi: Manohar Publishers and Distributors, 2000, p. 172.

14. Personal interview on 20/07/2014.

15. UN Department of Peacekeeping Operations, Disarmament, Demobilization and Reintegration of Ex-Combatants in a Peacekeeping Environment: Principles and Guidelines (1999), available at: https://peacekeeping.un.org/en/disarmament -demobilization-and-reintegration (Accessed on 01/04/2021).

16. Personal interview on 23/06/2013.

17. Personal interview on 24/07/2015.

18. Personal interview on 24/07/2015.

19. Personal interview on 23/06/2013.

20. Personal interview on 22/07/2014.

21. Personal interview on 22/07/2014.

22. Personal interview on 03/09/2014.

23. Cited in the report on "State of Human Rights in Jammu and Kashmir 1990–2005," published by *Jammu and Kashmir Coalition of Civil Society (JKCCS)*, The Bund, Amrita Kadal, Srinagar, pp. 260–61.

24. Personal interview on 29/07/2015.

25. Personal interview on 3/09/2014.

26. Personal interview on 22/07/2014.

27. Website Palestine for Kashmir at http://palestineforkashmir.wordpress.com/.

28. Website Electronic Intifada at http://electronicintifada.net/.

29. See, "Jammu and Kashmir reports highest internet shutdowns since 2012, 9 out of 27 reported in 2016 itself," *Indo-Asian News Service*, February 2017. Available at: https://www.india.com/technology/jammu-kashmir-reports-highest-internet -shutdowns-since-2012-9-out-of-27-reported-in-2016-itself-1822267/ (Accessed on 06/06/2021).

Chapter 5

Women's Agency Amid the Interplay of Masculinities

So far, I have discussed how military/militarized masculinities are constructed and enacted in the Kashmir conflict. They often compete with each other, and at the same time there exist multiple intersections, overlaps, and complexities in their performance. Amid such an interplay of masculinities, in this chapter I explore women's agency in the Kashmir conflict. I discuss women's agency in relation to these masculinities because the context in which women exercise their agency is shaped and informed by the complex masculine performances and vice versa. In the same light, it becomes important to study how women engage with and navigate the constructed narratives of femininity in a masculine environment. There co-exist several constructed narratives of femininity. For instance, Sikata Banerjee (2006) argues that, "Women enter this masculine environment through roles such as heroic mother, chaste wife and celibate warrior."

Masculinities and femininities are co-constructed by men and women alike and must be understood as dialectical and fluid categories. The study of women's choices and performed practices, in isolation from the ecosystem of gender performativity, often results in an incomplete understanding of women's position and roles and it works the other way as well. A deeper engagement of women's agency with masculinities will facilitate a nuanced analysis and also offer more insights into the gendered nature of both the conflict and the resistance movement. The feminist IR scholarship, both globally and, more specifically, in South Asia, has provided detailed and complex analysis of women's agency in conflict affected regions. Building on the existing conceptual frameworks provided by feminist IR scholars, I extend the study of women's agency to its engagement with the masculinities in conflict. There is a rich body of literature available on the women's roles and position in the Kashmir conflict.

Women's agency in the Kashmir conflict has been exercised in various capacities including, but also going beyond being a victim and/or a peace agent. Feminist literature on women's participation in the Kashmir conflict, in the last two decades, has focused on how women have gone beyond their victimhood or a "grieving" imagery. Such analysis has challenged the essentialist understanding of women's roles, but it perhaps seems to have fallen short to bring about the gray shades of women's agency and victimhood that do not fit into the binaries and frameworks of a victim-perpetrator and social actor. As opposed to such oversimplified versions of agency divided into victim-perpetrator-actor frameworks, a few scholars have complexified the analysis of women's agency in Kashmir by addressing the question of intersections with their Muslim identity (Malik, 2019) and tacit/creative ways in which they negotiate their spaces (Parashar, 2014). As an attempt to further provide a nuanced understanding of women's agency, I first explore the storytelling narratives and imposed discourses of motherhood on the one hand and resistance practices that women perform. I then highlight the dialectics between women's agency and masculinities. While studying women's agency, it is important to decipher who tells the story and for what ends, and how women's bodies are employed in these storytellings and what purposes they serve. It is then worthwhile to understand how women navigate through such discourses and exercise agency.

So, to provide a clear map of the chapter—in the first section, I assess the different mother narratives and imageries that are upheld by both the Indian state armed forces and the separatist/resistance projects in Kashmir. I argue that such frames and discourses are significant in not just confining femininity but also in reinforcing militarized masculinities. I discuss two aspects in this regard; first, how the circulation and representations of "Mother India," based on the Hindu conceptualizations of femininity, are significant elements in the construction of the idealized military masculinity; and second, the different maternal symbolisms available in the Kashmiri resistance movement such as those of the "kind," "sacrificing," and "grieving" mother (embodied by three women figures in the resistance Akbar Jehan, Zeenat [name changed] and Abida [name changed]) that intersect with the Muslim identity of women. The purpose of discussing such framing is not to deny the agency of women in any way, but to show the significance of the created mother symbols and their entanglements with masculinities in conflict and resistance.

In the second section, I look at how women in the Kashmir valley reinforce militant masculinities (both in the past and present) through various resistance practices. While navigating the imposed discourses on femininity, women find creative ways to be involved and participate in the resistance movement. This section entails the responses of women interviewees highlighting the diverse ways in which they exercise agency in the resistance movement, as well as how these practices provide an avenue for women to feel empowered. In the third section, building upon the discussion of demobilized masculinities (in chapter 4), I discuss how wives of former militants deal with both the victimizing experiences of their husbands and challenges of reintegration. In a similar light, through the narratives of the widows of Dardpora village and half-widows across different districts in the valley, I show women's navigation of everyday lived experiences in the varied absences of their husbands.

Women leaders in the resistance movement navigate the political patriarchal structures in different ways. Through my interviews with two prominent leaders, I discuss in the final section their unique and hybrid ways in both subverting and upholding patriarchy in Kashmiri resistance. As an extended part of this discussion, I also discuss the political agency of few women elected representatives of the Panchayat Halqas. These women may not be directly involved in the resistance movement; however, the village politics in Kashmir does not operate in isolation from the conflict and resistance dynamics. So, I explore how these women engage with everyday patriarchy and sometimes find themselves engulfed in the power struggle between the state and militant groups.

FEMININE/MATERNAL SYMBOLISMS IN MILITARISM AND RESISTANCE

The extent and limit of women's involvement in conflict and resistance is often determined by militarized actors to serve their own purposes. Women, no doubt, employ creative ways and means to negotiate the given spaces. However, in the context of masculine performativity, it becomes imperative to address the representation of women's agency that is framed by both the state militaries and militant/patriarchal resistance projects. I argue here that maternal symbolism and the portrayal of a good, virtuous, sacrificing, and dutiful mother is a powerful image to reinforce the military/militarized masculinities, both of state and nonstate actors.

Feminist IR scholarship has engaged theoretically with the idea of motherhood in multiple ways. I identify two dominant analyses primarily based on structural and agential aspects. In the first, motherhood is a narrative, a gender framing/representation, a myth, and an institution, and the second in which women exercise agency through motherhood and mothering practices, thus empowering themselves. On one hand, the theorizations of mothers and motherhood mainly emanate from Western feminist thought and pay less attention to creative negotiations practiced by women through motherhood. On the other hand, less conceptual exploration of motherhood is carried out in the feminist IR literature of the global south and tends to focus more on the activism of women as mothers.[1] I argue through the case of Kashmir, that a combination of both the structural and agential perspectives is significant in uncovering the deeper meanings attached to motherhood.

Bayard de Volo's (1998) reasons for motherhood being critical to the study of conflict are particularly relevant here: "first in the light of the widespread portrayal of women as nurturers, peacemakers, and givers of life, we must wonder how a nation (or any cultural group) manages to convince women to support their sons' entry into the war. Second, the construction of maternal identities for the war efforts has implications for women's place in postwar/conflict societies. Finally, maternal imagery is emotionally evocative and thus a powerful symbolic resource in garnering public support for war." In chapter 3, I discussed how these imageries strengthen the notion of masculinist protection (Young, 2003)[2] and are an integral part of the nationalist discourse in postcolonial contexts, especially with regard to the military practices in Kashmir. The popular depiction of "Mother India" can be traced to the importance of maternal presence within Hinduism. As Sharma (2018) argues, a number of Hindu female deities were worshipped as part of the ancient Indian society, and, despite the restriction of women's roles in Brahmanic tradition at the start of the Aryan civilization, the natural/primal energy remained symbolically feminine within the Hindu culture. Female mother deities are invoked for all natural calamities beyond the control of humankind (Nandy, 2005).[3] In relation to the Mother India imagery and its Hindu foundations, the origins can be traced to the idea of Mother Earth/land. In Hindu culture, land or earth is often referred to as a maternal form: "Dharti mata" or "Bhu Devi." In the cinematic presentations, especially visible in Bollywood movies, the soldiers often smear their foreheads with the mud invoking the imagery of "the motherland and her brave sons." However, the denotation of the Mother Earth as Mother India entailed a strong political movement, especially during the struggle for an independent nation. At the end of the nineteenth century, there were attempts at what Sen (2002) calls "reinventing the earth mother as the motherland." The gendered representation of the nation as Hindu mother—an object of worship, reverence, and protection—was first clearly articulated in Bankim Chandra Chatterjee/Chattopadhyay image of Bharat mata (Mother India) in the novel *Anandmath* (1882). It is said that the articulation inspired Bengal renaissance artist Abanindranath Tagore (also nephew of Rabindranath Tagore) who painted the first representation of "Bharat Mata" in 1905—a four-armed Hindu goddess wearing a saffron robe, holding a book, rice, garland of beads, and a white cloth. Before Abanindranath Tagore's painting, however, the image of Mother India first appeared in a play called *Bharatmata* by Kiranchandra Ray in 1873 (Get Bengal, 2021). Tagore's painting had more in common with Ray's image of Mother India, as weak, pale, and beaten by British colonizers as compared to the fierce goddess described in Bankim's words. Over a period of time, the graphics and imageries also went through transformations. In the modern version, for instance, Mother India is depicted as Hindu goddess Durga (although portrayed as secular) wearing a sari and holding an Indian flag. In this context, Banerjee (2006) explores two important cultural expressions of nation and manliness—Hindu soldier and warrior monk—disseminated by the Hindu nationalist organizations in India. She argues that women's bodies and roles in this Hindu nationalist masculine environment are reduced to national honor, and as such an embodiment that only works if women are "virtuous and chaste."

In the previous discussions, it was noted that Mother India is often invoked by the Indian army in their training practices as a motivational strategy. Narratives of soldiers (see chapter 3) point toward the significance of motherhood in the construction of masculinist protection imaginaries. The slogans "Bharat mata ki jai" (praise to Mother India), "We will protect our motherland," and pictures of India-as-mother are an important part of the training sessions of the Indian army. Furthermore, the projection of Hindu goddess imageries on the portrayed secular Mother India also shows the intersection of religious and nationalist discourses, along with highlighting the significance of maternal presence in the assertion of the idealized military masculinity. Especially during conflict situations, the good and the honorable mother (to be protected) narrative enables the strong reinforcement of violent forms of masculinity.

In addition to the powerful imagery of nation-as-mother, to fortify the military masculinity of the Indian state armed forces; there also simultaneously exists other motherhood narratives in the Kashmiri resistance movement to serve the masculinist projects of protection and violence. To fully understand women's political agency, it is important to make sense of the stories told through such mother narratives. Instead of focusing merely on the active participation of mothers in the Kashmir conflict, it is important to engage with the existing conceptualizations of motherhood discourse. The symbols of a "kind," "sacrificing," and "grieving" mother have been extensively used throughout the history of the Kashmiri resistance. The incorporation of mother role models in the resistance narrative provides authenticity and meaning to the movement. Three different yet significant symbols and imageries of motherhood projected upon Akbar Jehan (*Madar-e-Meherban,* the kind mother/mother of the community), Zeenat (name changed) (the sacrificing mother) and Abida (name changed) (the grieving mother), which have facilitated the resistance in different ways. Akbar Jehan's title of the kind mother created an active maternalist image of heroism and militant zeal (especially during the period of Sheikh Abdullah's incarceration) and also motivated more women to join the plebiscite movement.

Zeenat, the mother of the "martyred son" of Kashmir, is popularly portrayed as the sacrificing mother of Kashmir. People often give her salutations for producing the first Mujahid of Kashmir. Her reproductive role, however, is not just restricted to giving birth, but also to infuse bravery and masculinity in her son and his brothers. Many images and paintings of Zeenat holding pictures of killed militants are circulated by journalists in Kashmir and internationally. Abida represents the grieving image of the Kashmiri resistance. Her eighteen-year-old son was picked up by the Indian security forces and then disappeared. Abida's continued struggle to search for her son and providing support to other parents whose sons have disappeared, has been recognized in Kashmir and internationally. Internationally recognized for her feminist zeal, Abida is, however, the face of the "grieving mother" for the Kashmiri resistance movement. Locals in Kashmir call her relentless struggle to search for her son a result of being "grief-stricken."

In my interviews with Zeenat and Abida, I found that both the women were so much more than their symbolic portrayals in journalist writings and documentaries. Both in their different ways, had a strong political voice, passion, and enthusiasm for their respective struggles. Predominant writings and visuals, however, reduce their vibrant agential capacities to an imagery of "sacrificing" and "grieving" mother. The scripting of masculine and patriarchal projects tends to conceal the actual voice and agency of women like Zeenat and Abida, confining their roles to images and symbols to serve the goals of the patriarchal projects. The grieving mother image is extensively circulated in order to highlight the human rights violations of the Indian state. There is a wide presence of murals and pictures of mothers holding their sons' photographs in a protective manner. Such pictures depict the predicament of the mother's disappeared son and the psychological toll on the mother. On the contrary, the sacrificing mother image like that of Zeenat and other mothers of martyred sons is depicted as nonprotective, brave, courageous, and committed to the higher cause of Azadi (freedom). Different imageries are recruited to serve different purposes in the Kashmiri resistance. The mother narratives help, on the one hand, to increase the involvement of women in the movement and on the other hand, it also defined the bounds and confines of their activism. Alongside that, such portrayals also have an implied good and moral mother dimension for patriotic causes. The glorification and honor bestowed upon the sacrifices, resilience, and grief of mothers make it not only desirable for women to live up to this narrative, but it also strengthens the validation of the movement.

The above narratives are significant to understand how some stories are told in the conflict. However, what is also important to see is how women have engaged with these curated discourses and creatively exercise their agency. They have, within their confined roles of mothers, wives, and sisters, navigated political spaces and actively participated in the resistance movement. The rich history of women's involvement in the Kashmiri resistance since the Dogra rule can be seen in the earlier discussions (see chapter 2). Along with the gender roles, women also embrace their Muslim identity and consciousness and have claimed their space in resistance politics. As mentioned before, the oversimplified frameworks (for example, victim, perpetrators, and actors) to understand women's agency in Kashmir are questioned in different ways by contemporary feminist studies, as they delve deeper into the nuances and complexities involved. Building upon earlier studies on the intersection of women's agency with their Muslim identity and nuanced analysis of their creative conformity, the following part of the chapter further discusses how women's agency can be better understood by studying its relationship with the stories and narratives of the masculine environment in conflict. Some resistance practices discussed in the following section highlight the ways in which women deploy their agency to shape and reinforce militant masculinity in the Kashmir conflict.

RESISTANCE PRACTICES: WOMEN SHAPING AND REINFORCING MILITANT MASCULINITY

The boundaries between the "public" and "private" spheres often get fuzzy in a conflict affected society. The private sphere is politicized and sometimes even becomes a significant site of resistance. The mobilization of the domestic sector during a protracted crisis disputes any facile dichotomy between formal and informal spheres, and domestic and public domains. When a community is under attack domestic boundaries are shattered, revealing the illusory character of domesticity as the realm of private familial relations distanced from the spheres of formal politics (Peteet, 1986). In Kashmir, the politicization of the domestic sphere was particularly visible during the peak of the militancy movement when the domestic became an important space for the shaping of resistance practices. Some Kashmiri women pointed out in the interviews that their private lives remain politicized. For instance, Fatima (name changed) argued this:

> We are not living normal lives like other women in non-conflict zones. In normal circumstances, a woman cooks, nurtures, and takes care of her family, but in return feels protected by her husband. We have performed all household responsibilities as a political act—to prepare food for militants, tending to the wounded, educating our children to fight for the cause, and sacrificing our husbands and sons. The conflict has engulfed our private lives.[4]

From the interviews of women who actively participated in the resistance movement in the late 1980s, important resistance practices seem to have emanated in the private sphere. Instead of calling them "secondary" or "supporting" roles, as they're sometimes called in the existing conflict studies literature, I argue that these are crucial practices that shaped the resistance movement. Women provided shelter to the militants, tended to their wounds, helped them transfer weapons, prepared food for them, and some kept aside some money every month to buy rice and other food items just for the militants.

Shameena (name changed) mentioned that during the resistance movement of the late 1980s and early 1990s, she went to the farm, carrying arms, and gave those arms to some militants who came to collect them. Similarly, Zaheeda (name changed) pointed this out:

> Once a raid by the Indian Security forces happened in our locality, there were two militant brothers to whom I gave shelter and I protected them from security personnel and made the militant brothers stay with us, gave them food. Most of the Kashmiri people have helped the militants by giving food and shelter as we feel that they fought for our collective cause of freedom.[5]

During the same period, young women who had entered the marriageable age, desired to marry the militants, whom they viewed as "heroes." In social events such as marriages, young women sang couplets praising the militants such as *kalashmikov lagai balayai yenav ladayat path fairaleh* ("don't give up this fight for freedom, I shower my life on this kalshnikov"), and "main mujahidov behan paraie hideouts" (O my beloved militant, I will wait for you at the hideout). (Sobhrajani, 2008). There was competition among women supporters to compose pre-militancy couplets. Marrying a militant was a matter of pride in the whole village. Sadiya (name changed), a wife of an ex-militant pointed this out:

> My husband's eldest brother had picked up arms in the late 1980s. The entire village was so proud of him. I was not married to Altaf (name changed) then. We met at a wedding in my village. All young girls sang songs to motivate men to join the movement for Azadi. I remember composing a couplet too. After a few days, Altaf's mother met my family to talk about our marriage. She also told us that Altaf wanted to join the movement. I was so happy and proud to hear that. I always wanted to marry a man who was brave to take up the cause of Azadi. We cared more about the cause.[6]

Women who married militants said that it was a great honor to marry someone who was brave enough to take up arms to fight for the cause of Kashmir. Some women admitted that they still kept pictures of militants they loved, since they were the heroes. The politicization of the domestic is also evident in the reproductive politics, embodied in the "mother of martyr"; the maternal sacrifice of a son is the supreme political act, and the mother becomes the symbol of trauma of exile and resistance, as discussed in the previous section (Neugebauer, 1998).

As a political practice, mothering is significant in the Kashmiri resistance because women's involvement as mothers provides validation and legitimacy to the armed militancy and the resistance movement. Women's deployment of agency as mothers may not be subversive of patriarchy, but their negotiation of spaces within the confines of the mother narrative is a significant form of agency that requires attention. Mothering practices in Kashmir have, to a great extent helped in shaping and reinforcement of militant masculinities.

Historically, women adopted mothering practices to assert their voice in Kashmiri resistance and politics. They shaped the masculine ideals of Mujahid (militant heroes) during the peak of militancy in the 1990s. Young women's enthusiasm to reproduce militants both literally and symbolically was clearly visible in the popular slogan, *Pakistan Jaayenge, Do Roti Khaayenge, pet mein mujahid leke ayenge* ("We will go to Pakistan, eat two breads and come back pregnant with a militant child") (Parashar, 2011).

Women also encouraged men to take up arms and decorated their militant sons as bridegrooms with henna on their hands and garlands around their necks, sending them to get *Azadi* (freedom) as the bride. An ex-militant Javed, recalls,

> I was reluctant to pick up arms, but the time was such that there was a wave of desire for freedom in the hearts of all Kashmiris in the valley. My mother motivated me and said—"You need to fight for azadi for Kashmir." I didn't want to leave my family, my mother motivated me to join the tehriq. The day I went I was decorated like a groom. The entire village was singing folk songs of pride. It was the same story everywhere.[7]

As mothers, they shaped and continue shaping the masculine ideals of the Mujahid (the militant warrior) in the Kashmir conflict (Agarwal, 2018). Singing songs of martyrdom, glory, and pride at funerals and giving emotional speeches, they also infused masculinity in the dead bodies of militant sons to keep the resistance movement alive. Funerals have always been an important site through which women exercise agency and claim their collective space in the resistance movement. Similarly, rallies such as those organized by the Muslim Khwateem Markaz (MKM) were also significant spaces for the women to actively participate in the resistance. Women working in MKM went to strengthen the morale of the mothers whose sons are killed by the security forces. The gathered women would sing songs, raising slogans of freedom, and celebrate martyrdom instead of mourning.

I also conducted some interviews with mothers from a village, which is also known as the "Gaza of Kashmir." According to the locals living in this village, the Indian state armed forces had blockaded this village, cut electricity and water, and opened fire on civilians after the stone-pelting movement in 2010. Some young boys were shot, and the village has its own martyr's graveyard. Each grave had a few lines written in the glory of the martyred (Agarwal, 2018). The interviewed mothers who lost their sons in this village strongly endorsed the cause of freedom.

One of them said, "It was the will of God that he came in our life and it his will to take him back. I have no regrets about whatever happened. I just feel proud that my son is a martyr and I am his mother."[8] Similarly, a mother from the same village mentioned that "God had willed it so," and if her two living sons also chose the path of Azadi, she will wholeheartedly support them in this good cause. Women seem to critically engage with the victimizing experiences and refuse to be subjugated by them. The affirmation of motherhood enables them to feel intimately involved in the resistance against what they find an oppressive subjection. Religion also facilitates their involvement and provides an effective coping mechanism. The ideas of "acceptable death" and of "meaningful" (rather than useless) suffering serve to cope with the rage and grief for those whose lives were unnecessarily lost or taken. The ways in which women shape militant masculinity and strengthen resistance movement as mothers constitute the exercise of political agency. Motherhood, as a political practice, clearly creates a pathway for women's active involvement in the resistance movement. Practicing mothering in conflict is a political act, an expression of making strong political choices in the given sociopolitical

Figure 5.1 Martyr's graveyard of a village (also known as Gaza of Kashmir), Kashmir. The graves of all young resisters who lived in this village and were killed by the Indian security forces. Photo: Amya Agarwal

Figure 5.2 Poetry on the grave of a young boy killed in firing by the security forces, Photo: Amya Agarwal[9]

context. Another point that becomes clear from studying women's agency through resistance practices is that like in the case of male survivors of violence, there is no "point of arrival" where women transform from being victims to agents. Victimhood and agency go hand in hand and sometimes victimhood may provide a potential pathway to resistance. In this case, it may be useful to clarify that by victimhood I mean as perceived by the survivors themselves and not superimposed by the masculine projects. Scholars have questioned the gendered opposition of agency and victimhood that typically characterizes the analysis of women's coping strategies in war zone (Utas, 2005). Krystalli (2020) also articulates the need to incorporate a simultaneous analysis of victimhood and agency, (without polarizing them into binaries) succinctly: "Taking victimhood seriously requires moving away from a view of it as always synonymous with vulnerability or lack of agency or as entirely reduced to the experience of victimization." Similarly, studying women's agency in Kashmir, thus requires going beyond a dichotomy of vulnerabilities/victimhood and agency, by focusing on the nuances of women's roles and tacit intersections of their agency with patriarchy.

CONFRONTING ABSENCE, PRESENCE AND LIMINALITY: THE AGENCY OF WIVES OF FORMER MILITANTS, WIDOWS AND HALF-WIDOWS

In chapter 4, I discussed the demobilized masculinities of former ex-militants and the challenges they face after their return to civilian life, in the form of social alienation, detention, lack of job skills, economic insecurities, and feelings of inadequacy in relation to the violence and torture they underwent. Their past experiences of violence and their present victimization as civilians have also had a profound impact on women's roles, positions, and agency. For instance, when some young men left their wives and young children behind to join the militancy movement, women had to assume the nontraditional roles of being the breadwinner and the protector of the family. On their return, the reintegration of former militants into civilian life was equally challenging for women. Due to the long absence, it became hard for some families of the returning former militants to recalibrate themselves to the change. Also, due to their physical incapacities, some former militants were unable to work and stayed at home, which resulted in the inability to return to expected gender roles. As discussed before, the frustration and aggression of ex-combatants along with the reality of domestic issues, sometimes manifested in domestic violence. Women had to grapple with both the absence and the return of their husbands in different ways. Some of the narratives of former militants show how the gender roles went through a reversal on their return and the domestic challenges that surfaced as a result.

Ghulam Amjad (name changed) was a supporter of the militancy and later became an informer for a militant group during the peak of the armed resistance. He remained outside his village for long periods, during which time his wife had to earn for the family. He said this:

> My wife started farming and would also take care of the house. I returned to village but had to remain underground; but soon I was arrested while crossing the border. After I was released, I desperately looked for a job but did not find any job despite being a graduate. Finally, I started weaving carpets in Srinagar but since I wanted to be with family, so I returned to the village. Now I spend the whole day with the children, while my wife works at a farm.

Nazima Sheikh (name changed), a former militant's ex-wife, for instance, pointed out:

> After he returned, he was a different man. He stayed aloof. He was not so involved in family life. I had spent most years of my life taking care of children and earning without much support. I had expected things to get better after he

came back. It became worse and he ended our marriage. So, I decided to remarry and now at least I live a dignified life.

With little support, the wives of former militants assumed nontraditional roles during the absence of their husbands. Despite the many difficulties they confronted, they managed to raise their children and fulfill work responsibilities. Even during the return of their husbands, most of the interviewed women continued earning and taking care of the households. Due to the marital discord and other domestic issues that arose on the return of few former militants, like in the case of Nazima, some women even decided to leave their husbands. The children of the former militants were also conscious of their mothers' increased difficulties due to both the absence and return of their fathers. However, the majority of wives of interviewed former militants had accepted their husbands' return, despite the challenges of reintegration. Apart from the domestic struggles of the wives of the former militants returning to civilian life, there were also women whose husbands never returned from Pakistan-administered Kashmir. Shoaib Ali, a nineteen-year-old whose father joined the militancy movement but never returned, pointed out that

My father left my mother and family when I was just born, to join the freedom movement. My father was educated till the twelfth standard but he had no job, so he joined the armed struggle. My mother took care of me and also earned money and worked as a laborer. My grandfather had some money that he gave to my mother and that money was used for my education. I am a graduate, but I have no job since there are not many job opportunities, even for educated people. I am still looking for a job. My father never returned; he must have married there leaving us in poverty. I cannot see my mother work as a laborer. I feel I am grown up enough to earn for her, but I feel ashamed of not being able to earn.[10]

The absence-and-presence dynamics can be further extended to understand the agency of the widows and half-widows in Kashmir. Some women whose militant-husbands were killed during encounters with the Indian army have navigated the absence in multiple ways. These are particularly visible in the experiences of the widows of Dardpora village in Kupwara district. The name of this village means the "abode of pain" and is situated in the same border district as Kunan Poshpora, the village where a mass rape by the Indian security forces had occurred in 1991. Dardpora has witnessed numerous deaths of youth and the village has around 133 widows and 444 orphans.[11] Most of the killed were militants shot by the Indian army and some died due to internal rivalry within and between the militant groups Al-Barq and Hizbul Mujahideen. Being extremely close to the borders, it is heavily militarized and has seen a considerable loss of human life since the peak of armed resistance. Many of the widows in the Dardpora chose not to remarry and face major financial constraints with very little support from the government or NGOs. Most of them mentioned the support they received from Bait-ul-maal system.[12] Following narratives of the widows show the different ways in which they dealt with life after the death of their husbands:

Shanti Begum (name changed):

> My husband used to teach students at a mosque. He was taken away by the military in Kralpora in 1996. But no one knew that. At 3 a.m. during night, villagers heard firing, but no one went outside. In the morning, two men came and said that in a shop there were some blood stains and meat pieces. But when people moved to Kralpora, half of my husband's dead body (lower part) was missing.
>
> Villagers buried half of his body. Ever since that day I have taken all the responsibilities of home like a man. I sometimes go to other people's houses to clean in order to earn. The villagers also helped with Bait-ul-Maal. Widow welfare scheme is only Rs 200, what is that worth? I have three children but none of them could study above class fifth due to the mental trauma they went through after their father's death.
>
> I am out of the house all day, I return late. My elder son used to take care of the younger children. I have led a difficult life, many women in this village live like this. Some NGOs like Yateem Trust often come to our village to help us financially.[13]

Tasmeena/Simarjeet (name changed):

> My husband was a militant. He was killed during torture, as he was captured during an encounter in Tangwadi. I had run away from my parents' house in Punjab to marry my husband. But now I can't even go back to their place. It has been ten years since my husband died. I have three sons and three daughters. I sent two of my daughters to Rahat Ghar (orphanage). My cousin-brother from Punjab came and bought roof sheets for me and people from NGO came to build three rooms for me. But, other than that I have to earn every single day to feed my children. I do that sometimes by begging for money and also indulging in community help. My brother-in-law comes to my house and pressures me to marry him and even beats me up when I refuse. When my children were very small, I used to leave them every day in the house alone and go begging from one house to another. I had no choice as I had no support from my husband's family after he died.[14]

Shehnaz Khan (name changed):

> My husband was a militant and was trained in Pakistan. He was killed in Panzgam, as he had weapons. After his death, I have on my own raised four children. The only I support I got was from the community Bait-ul-Maal system. My son is suffering from kidney problems, and it costs two thousand rupees every time I get some treatment done. I used to repair used clothes and then sell

them, that is how I earned money. My husband passed away just five years after marriage and my children were very small then. I still remember locking them up all together in one room and going to earn money. What else could I do? I had to earn money, how else would I have fed them? With God's grace, all my children have studied 'til twelfth grade, and I am thankful to God. I had some land that belonged to my husband, which I sold to educate them. I had to be both father and mother to my children.[15]

While acknowledging their victimizing experiences and painful circumstances, women have simultaneously embraced nontraditional roles and despite only little support, found ways to educate their children and earn their livelihood. They have found different ways to become financial independent. Saima (name changed) is teaching school children how to read and write. She is determined to get through although she also admits that women have a harder time working, "because they have to do so much housework."[16] Some women have learned Kashmiri embroidery, weaving, and other skills so that they can find some means to earn a living. NGOs help the widows in setting up small businesses of embroidery, carpet weaving, and shops.

Despite the serious challenges, women have also exercised agency in different ways to support the militarized resistance. For instance, some provided aid to the militants while others educated their children about the resistance movement. As one of the widows pointed out, "My husband was a freedom fighter. He was very passionate about freedom. He was killed in a crackdown by the Indian army. I was pregnant when he died. My son was born, and every day I have taught him about getting Azadi (freedom). I have instilled the same passion for freedom, he will pick up arms and take revenge for us."[17] Similarly, another widow felt anger toward the Indian armed forces and expressed her strong support for the militancy movement. "I had nothing to live for. I helped the militants if they needed it. I gave them shelter, I cooked for the militants. It was they who told me that they will take revenge for me. May the militants secure the Azadi that we dream of."[18] The widows in this village do not express their support for the resistance movement explicitly by protesting on the streets or singing songs of martyrdom and glory at the funerals. In the past, they exercised their agency in other ways, like providing aid and shelter to militants and educating their children about the history and significance of the resistance movement; alongside explaining the reason for their anger toward the Indian state armed forces.

There are also women in Kashmir who navigate a liminal space between the absence and presence of their husbands. These women are commonly known as half-widows, as their husbands disappeared for years and never returned. A prominent human rights activist defines "enforced disappearance as a part of the larger policy of repression followed by the state in its efforts to curb militancy in Kashmir. However, a large number of civilians, students, political activists and militants have disappeared in custody of the state."[19] In 2011, APDP estimated about 1,500 half-widows, however, the Jammu and Kashmir Coalition of Civil Society (JKCCS) claimed that this figure is quite conservative, and the number of half-widows could be more than 8,000.[20] The Islamic Human Rights Commission also claims that there were 1,500 half-widows in 2010–2011.[21]

The cases of disappearances documented by the APDP reveal a common pattern: the forces enter and search a house and take the eldest son stating that they need to question him. This son is never seen again. In most cases, wives and other family members who go looking for their loved one are sent from one military base to another, one jail to another each suggesting some clue at the next. The family members only keep going from one place to another in vain and do not find any trace of their loved one. For instance, Hena (name changed) was a half-widow in 2003. Her thirty-five-year-old husband, Muneer (name changed), worked as a mason. They lived in their Baramulla House with their four children, Muneer's parents, his two sisters, and four brothers. Men of the state armed forces knocked at their door. The male members of the family were separated from the women and the children. Muneer, the eldest brother was escorted out of the house. The family was told that he would return the next day, after some questioning. Eight years later, Muneer has still not returned. Hena said,

> We went everywhere. We recognize the men who came that night, we even know their names. We went and asked them, and they refused to tell anything about my husband. My husband was taken from our family sitting room. Yet those men roam around free, and I am neither a married woman nor a widow. . . . I am just waiting.[22]

As wives of men who have disappeared, half-widows face various economic, social, and emotional insecurities. Most of the disappearances have happened in the rural areas, where women enjoy way less economic and social independence. The uncertain nature and duration of the absence open women to scrutiny and policing by their society as well as threats, extortion, and manipulation by those in external positions of power. For instance, a class of messengers has made a business out of taking money (up to hundreds and thousands of rupees) from families to convey information from the captors. In their desperation, many half-widows also visit Sufi saints (*peer*, *fakirs*, *darweshs*), make offerings at the Sufi shrines and some even patronize fortune tellers (*Times of India*, 2011).

Sana (name changed), a resident of Srinagar is a half-widow. She said this:

What do I want? One meeting. If he's alive, just show me. If he's dead, tell me where his body is. When I go back to the Police or the Army, the officials leer like I am available, like I have to remind them that I am there about my missing husband.[23]

Nasleema (half-widow) (name changed):

My husband disappeared back in 2011. I often visit the Human Rights Commission and even other governmental institutions in search of my husband. I have even gone to the army camps in search of him. I feel if he was alive, he would have returned.

When my husband disappeared, the children were very young. I brought them up. I got some support from the community and some from my brother. Most of the times I used to sell livestock in order get support. My husband's family does not support me at all. I had put my sons in a Jamat-run charity school that provides free education. I got supported from my in-laws eight years ago. My health had really deteriorated after my husband disappeared, and the doctor had advised me not to do any hard task, but there is no other way to feed my children. My elder son tells me that earlier he had expectations that his father might return, but now he feels that his father is dead. He often tells me that from now on only you are my father.[24]

The interviews conducted with half-widows showed that they are mostly economically dependent on their in-laws. However, some either leave or are forced to leave their in-law's home. While deciding matters of inheritance, the disappeared sons are mostly counted out as non-existing and their children's inheritance becomes zero. Also, without an official declaration of the husband's death, the half-widows are not entitled to ex gratia payment by the state. Even the issuance of the ration cards, transfer of husband's property, or bank accounts are closed to half-widows, since these procedures require the death certificates.[25] Most of the half-widows do not contemplate remarriage, believing that they will eventually have some information about their husbands. However, for those who want to remarry, social stigmas regarding remarriage remain strong, while religious interpretations of the rules around remarriage remain contested. Even pursuing judicial remedies for the half-widows is a tiring process, and their problems are compounded rather than addressed by the legal and administrative remedies that are available. Delays, costs, and harassment of the process of availing remedies is deterrent enough for most and lead to further dejection. Very few half-widows approach the lawyers. For instance, H. U. Salati, advocate in Jammu and Kashmir High court pointed out this:

Lack of formal education, economic constraints, geographic distances from Srinagar and the fears of further victimization, retaliation and mutilation of memories of the disappeared—only about 5% of the half-widows in Kashmir in fact pursue legal recourse. Even for those who pursue these remedies, justice remains elusive.[26]

While women are directly impacted by the victimization of their male family members and also feel constrained due to social expectations, their victimhood and agency go hand in hand. Like the wives of former militants and the widows of Dardpora, the half-widows also find ways to address their victimhood and develop their own coping mechanisms to deal with the absence of their husbands. Some have found employment in farms, orchards, crafts businesses; some find financial, emotional, and childcare support through the local Kashmiri NGOs.

NAVIGATING PATRIARCHAL STRUCTURES IN POLITICS: COMPLICIT AND SUBVERSIVE FORMS OF AGENCY

Women holding positions of power in Kashmir navigate the patriarchal structures in the political sphere in diverse ways. Some of these experiences problematize liberal, second-wave feminist notions—that awarding more equitable representation to women in the public sphere doesn't necessarily result in a gender-sensitive exercise of power and that women can and do also uphold and reinforce patriarchy. Others show women using their positions to advance women-related issues through their political agendas and decision-making. Taking the role of women in the Kashmir conflict as the departure point, in this section I seek to explore how women navigate the patriarchal structures in the political sphere through exercising both complicit and subversive forms of political agency. The point is not to simply categorize women's agency as complicit and subversive of patriarchy, but rather to show the plurality of ways in which agency is exercised creatively to navigate patriarchy. Here, I explore the different ways in which women leaders in the Kashmiri resistance such as Haniya (name changed) and Zoya (name changed) make sense of their interactions with patriarchy and masculinized practices in the conflict. Toward the end of the section, I also briefly discuss the experiences of a few elected representatives of village Panchayat Halqas (*local self-government*) to understand how they engage with patriarchal expectations of both the state and non-state actors. While their experiences may not be directly related to the resistance movement, however, their agency also operates within the context and dynamics of the conflict and deserves to be told and heard.

Haniya: Navigating and Upholding Patriarchy through Her Reflections on Muslim Identity

Haniya is a prominent figure of the Kashmiri resistance movement, and her activism is quite complex to say the least. Feminists have long debated and contested the nature of her political involvement in the resistance movement. Some call her Islamic feminist, while some criticize her activism as exacerbating the marginalization of Kashmiri women. Her organization has also made global headlines as "women jihadi" in international media. Instead of focusing on the preexisting labels of "feminist" or a "soft terrorist"; it may be more useful from a gender studies perspective, to understand Haniya's agency through her engagement with patriarchy, in both confronting and upholding it.

In my interview with her, Haniya talked about her religious curiosity in her younger days and the dissatisfaction she felt with the expectations of being a "Syed." The Syed are upper-class Muslims who trace their direct lineage to the Islamic prophet. They are expected to follow and reproduce social hierarchies and reinforce their elite status. Along with her disagreement with the social role of the clan she belonged to, she also confronted patriarchy at home when her brother opposed her decision to go out of Kashmir for education. In those moments of sadness, she was reflective on her purpose of life and started reading *Khawateen ke Dilon ki baatein* (The stories of the hearts of women). The book had the story of Maryam Jameel, a Jewish woman who converted to Islam, which inspired her immensely and opened a new way to understand Islam. She mentioned this:

> that is when I realized that Islam is so important and until then I was only performing an obligatory duty towards Islam. I read the Quran again, did my first proper *wazu* and *namaz* and started covering my whole body. My father and my family were not very happy with my decision. That day I cried a lot in front of my father. I told him that "you have been such a wonderful father, but you never told us the real Islam and its teachings."[27]

Islam's assertion as being political was especially striking for Haniya: "Islam is a way of life. It provides guidance to Muslims on how to live. Islam is also a guiding force for politics. They are not separate."[28] She mentioned that she regularly listened to Radio Pakistan which broadcasted a program on the teachings of Quran in 1984. Furthermore, in her quest to learn more about Islam, she joined religious classes organized by Jamat-i-Islami. Disappointed by Jamat's lack of a clear position on Kashmiri politics, its soft stance toward the Indian state, and the glorification of Sheikh Abdullah's politics, she left the classes. Subsequently, she embarked on the journey of studying religion herself. She was offered a job by a Darsgah in her neighborhood to teach the Quran to children. However, she eventually left the job and decided to educate women about their rights in Islam and their role in the political struggle.

Haniya saw Islam's potential in radically bringing a change in the political life of people in Kashmir and shaped women's politics across Kashmir. Haniya started the first women's Darsgah in 1985, which aimed at imparting religious education to women. Haniya along with her students took stand on issues around the exploitation of Kashmiri women by the state and questioned gendered expectations through the teachings of Islam. For their activism and protest, they received public attention, were applauded in a local newspaper, and became a prominent group. Women from the middle and lower classes joined the movement as their Darsgah grew across several districts in Kashmir. Haniya's lectures were recorded and circulated for wider public consumption. They vehemently opposed the commodification of women and applied black paint on pictures and posters of Bollywood actresses. According to Haniya,

> I wanted women to know about the tenets of Islam and the status accorded to them. In 1987, our organization called upon women to come out and protest against the portrayal of women in the nude in advertising. This is no progress! Later, when the freedom struggle picked up, I questioned the accession of Kashmir. As a result, my office was raided and sealed.[29]

During the late 1980s, Haniya and other women from the group started protesting against the circulation of "immoral activities" in the form of "modern" traditions in Kashmir. The organization started enforcing a restrictive code of conduct, particularly on women. There were some journalist reports that mentioned the imposition of diktats and moral policing pursued by women activists under the leadership of Haniya. Valentine's day cards and posters were burnt and raided liquor shops were raided by the women activists (Parashar, 2011). It was noted that Haniya's organization launched door-to-door campaigns to make women appreciate the importance of the veil. This campaign was also accompanied by warnings of the dire consequence of defiance.

With the rise of armed resistance in Kashmir and Haniya's explicit support for militancy and a firm anti-state stand, the government raided her offices and sealed them. Her organization was banned in 1990, after which Haniya was mostly underground or in detention. Haniya has been incarcerated by India's national investigation agency on multiple occasions, most recently in 2018. Her husband is serving life imprisonment on charges of involvement of the murder of a Kashmiri pandit human rights activist in 1992. Haniya's choices, and her way of exercising agency, were informed by her reflection of Islam shaped by early experiences with patriarchy. Her agency can be seen as religious where she adopted political Islam as a foundation to carve out the identity, rights, and participation of a Kashmiri woman. Several women who joined Haniya's organization found an avenue to be involved in the resistance in their own right as a woman within a male-dominated, conservative society. This identity also provided an imagined legitimate space for women to support violence. However, on the other hand, the narrative of the "political Muslim-Kashmiri woman" formulated by Haniya reproduced and upheld patriarchy through the imposition of codes and behavior toward all Kashmiri women. The women who joined her organization in the late 1980s found a significant religious pathway to enter the resistance movement in the late 1980s; however, their activism involved the violent control of women's femininity, which was not very different from the militant groups that issued rules and warnings regarding dress codes and behavior in the 1990s. Thus, Haniya's agency reflects both confrontation with patriarchal structures but also a strong reinforcement and affirmation of patriarchal practices.

ZOYA'S HYBRID RESISTANCE: FIGHT AGAINST PATRIARCHY COMBINED WITH THE ASPIRATION OF POLITICAL FREEDOM

There are examples of women leaders in Kashmiri resistance movement who have entered the domain of politics on their own, without the privilege of a political family background or the help of any male relatives. One such example is that of Zoya who used politics as a platform to bring forth freedom-related struggle combined with women-related issues such as dowry and domestic abuse that are often overlooked in conflict-affected contexts. Zoya is the head of the only women's organization that comes under the umbrella of a prominent alliance of social and religious organizations. While talking to Zoya, she argued that her decision to enter politics was to bring her struggle for women's issues to a political platform. She said this:

> Ever since I was in college I used to be actively involved in campaigning for women's rights. I remember, there was a dowry death in my village, and we formed a Women's Welfare Association in our College, even pandit women joined this association. It was an all-inclusive women's movement. I became a part of politics not for any other reason but to bring this movement on a political platform.[30]

Although being a Kashmiri Muslim, Zoya does not give much importance to veiling. She pointed out that a veil simply implies *jism pe libas is pur-dah* (clothing that does not reveal the contours of the body). She works on women-related issues through her organization and often stressed about the importance of the role of women in conflict and the need for the women's issues to find a political platform. And hence, inclusion of women in the political decision-making is extremely important according to her. Because the political system was highly masculinized, she pointed out that she had, on a number of occasions, sought to include women-related issues at the center stage of party policy-making. According to Zoya, her fellow party leaders had reservations regarding the representation of women in decision-making processes/structures. There have been instances where she even fought with her fellow party workers to debate issues concerning women. She argued the following:

> There is nothing written about women quota as members and in decision-mak-ing body in the constitution of the party. The condition there is quite abysmal and pathetic, women's voices are ignored and their political participation and representation in the decision-making body is minimal. In a meeting, I remem-ber fighting with a fellow male leader to include women in decision making. I strongly feel women have to be a part of decision-making. Most of the times women's issues do not find a place in the party agenda and that infuriates me.[31]

Even though her attempts were futile, Zoya tried to subvert masculine politics in her own ways. According to her, when the women's organization under her leadership had proposed in 1995 that ex-militants should be "persuaded" to marry the raped women to set an example for the Kashmiri youth, the idea was rejected by the party leaders. Later, during the party's hunger strike in New Delhi in 1998 to highlight the issue of rapes in Kashmir, ironically, not a single woman was present. This women-specific issue was talked about by men only because the leaders did not believe that the presence of their women members was necessary. When asked about why women do not find a place in the decision-making body of the party, the popular separatist leader of the party replied, saying that "our duty is to keep women safe; they can be arrested, manhandled, and picked up like other leaders."[32]

Zoya's experiences of being in the prison for five years, in her book, also shows the uncaring attitude of party's male leaders in helping her get released, when she was arrested in Delhi, and convicted under the prevention of the Terrorism Act (POTA). She noted that her male colleague was sent a lawyer from the party, but she wasn't, despite her family requesting the party leaders to take action for her. Her ordeal in the prison and abandonment by the party she had worked for, however, did not deter her from political activism.

Women like Zoya through her work in the women's organization and have taken up issues and concerns of widows and half-widows in Kashmir. They go to the households of such women, listen to their experiences, give them strength, and record such cases and seek intervention on their behalf in the party agenda. Their book titled *Our Widows*, published in 2010, documents eighty-six cases of widows who they had planned to rehabilitate through donations received by them. Zoya had also formed an association for prisoners of Kashmir families and was involved in collecting books and other reading material for distributing among the Kashmiris who are imprisoned in various jails across India. When asked about her views on creating an independent women's group, separate from the party, for taking up women's issues and concerns, she answered:

> Our organization has suffered a lack of unity due to which it went through a split. However, through dedicated work we have succeeded in providing a unique identity to our organization. But the trouble is that in the party, women's concerns are missing. It is my dream to have a women's organization to be independent of the party leadership that only focuses on issues related to women and that aims at uplifting the condition of women. However, as women in Kashmir we can never be a part of an organization that is separate from the movement for freedom or from the movement for religion.[33]

The political agency of Zoya, cannot be seen in isolation from the resistance movement and aspirations for political freedom. For instance, a rally organized by women workers visited a woman's house whose militant son was killed by the security forces. The motive of the rally was to provide moral strength to the mother; however, such rallies also become significant platforms for mobilizing women for the political resistance against the state violence. The combination of both the women's issues and strong resistance sentiments in her struggle, display a peculiar form of agency. Sometimes these elements become incompatible; however, she continues to choose both in the possible and available ways.

Mixed Agency of Elected Representatives in Panchayat Halqas

The exercise of women's agency in navigating patriarchal political structures is different in rural areas. I conducted interviews with a few elected women representatives (*panch and sarpanch*) of the local governing bodies called *panchayat halqas*, in different blocks in Baramulla, Anantnag, and Pulwama districts. From the perspective of political representation, I look at how on the one hand they're able to fulfill (or not) their expected duties in an otherwise male-dominated domain; and on the other hand, grapple with the demands of the armed resistance movement.

Empowering grassroots political institutions has been long-standing goal of the National Conference and emphatically mentioned as such in the "New Kashmir Manifesto." This ideal was incorporated into the state's constitution, which made it obligatory for the state to take steps to organize village panchayats and endow them with such powers and authority as maybe necessary to enable them to function as a unit of self-government (Kumar, 2012). In 2013, an amendment made to the Jammu and Kashmir Panchayati Raj Act of 1989, whereby, the principle of 33 percent of seat reservation for women was extended to the Block Development Councils.

Previous studies evaluating the representation of women in local bodies in the Kashmir valley suggest that while the women members in panchayat halqas, such as Kulgam and Baramulla districts, have the potential to become good leaders and play a key role in grassroots politics, they are unable to do so as decision making remains a male dominated domain and they also faced threats of being killed by the militants.[34] It was also reported in these local studies, that women's interests are often not seen as an integral part of the overall constituency interests which the representatives need to take up. Also, panchayat politics play a significant role in defining the interests and the priorities of the representative, but gender issues as such are generally not a priority.

However, my interviews with the elected women representatives in the panchayat halqas across the mentioned districts suggest a mix of performance. While many women panchs fought elections on the directions given by their male relatives and hardly attended any of the panchayat meetings, there were some women panchs and sarpanchs who were proactive in addressing the issues in their villages, attended all the meetings of the panchayat, and even had a strong say in its decision-making structures and processes.

Sahina (name changed), a panch elected from Pulwama, took part in elections only because her husband was also a panch, and he wanted her to take part in elections. She confessed that she had never attended any of the panchayat meetings and nor did she know anything about the developmental work happening in her village. Similarly, Rubina (name changed) from Anantnag, fought panchayat elections because her father asked her to do so. She too had never attended the panchayat meeting nor was she aware of the quantum of funds allotted for different development work in her village. Another Panch, Hamila begum (name changed) from the same block also pointed out that she was not very involved in the panchayat activities and had fought panchayat elections so that she could earn some money and get her own house constructed, which according to her, never happened. She said:

We were living under extreme impoverished conditions, so I thought becoming a panch will benefit me. We don't have any agricultural land or any other economical support. My husband is a daily wage earner. That's why I fought elections with the hope that we would get some monetary benefit and have my house constructed. But that didn't happen.[35]

Some other elected women panchs and sarpanchs in different blocks in Baramulla and Anantnag, however, played a proactive role in the panchayat affairs. Some of them had a strong hold on the household resources and had a significant say in the decision-making both in their homes and in the panchayat. Even despite the constant threat from the militants, they consciously chose to take part in political decision-making processes in their village panchayats. Asiya B (name changed), a panch from Baramulla, pointed out that there was a dire need for women to participate in decision-making since men alone could not take good decisions for the entire village community and there were also problems in procuring funds since men are not seen as trustworthy by the authorities. Similarly, the husband of Raha B (name changed), a female sarpanch argued that

It has been easier for women to receive funds, since they are more trusted by the government. Sometimes, when due to corruption, the money for village development doesn't reach the panchayat, so women fight to get the money and they succeed in getting it back. With women being elected there is more accountability.[36]

Apart from the advantage of the trust in procuring funds, some elected women representatives have been actively involved in the decision making for their villages, such as allocation of funds for development and women-related issues such as domestic violence and welfare of widows. While elite women representatives in formal politics at the state level grapple with the structural constraints of patriarchy in the political sphere; women involved in the panchayats are relatively more independent. For instance, Rohini (name changed), a female panch pointed this out:

I am always present in the meetings of the Panchayat. In fact, all the women panchs in our village attend the Gram Sabha and meetings. Although the final decision is taken by Sarpanch, all decisions involve discussions that happen between the Panchs and Sarpanch at our home, we have tea and even women members are present.[37]

Similarly, Raha B said this:

There are six male panchs and two female panchs working under me. Whatever
be the problem, I take the decision after consulting the panchs. If I don't like the
suggestions of panchs I make my own decision. None of panchs whether male
and female, have any binding force over me. I visit various government officials
myself, there is no shadow decision making.[38]

Notwithstanding their illiteracy, these women elected representatives deal
with a number of women-related issues such as domestic violence and rehabilitation of widows in their villages. For instance, Malsooma Akhtar (name
changed), the deputy sarpanch in a block, pointed out that there are many
women in the villages that complain of being beaten up by their husbands
and in-laws, for which the Gram Sabha is held, and the cases are resolved by
the female members of the Halqa. She added that normally these cases would
go to the police stations but with the election of the female members in the
panchayat, these have been resolved at the village level only. Malsooma's
(name changed) husband also mentioned that some widows in the village
whose husbands had been killed in the conflict, and Kaifiya (name changed),
along with the other female panchs and the sarpanch, had been successful
in procuring funds for constructing a few houses for the widows. Pointing
toward a house in the village, he said that "the house has been built for Nazia
(name changed), a widow and her children, through the funds that the women
representatives procured, and three other such widows have also been provided houses."[39]

Nazia added:

I have been helped a lot by the Panchayat Halqa, they have helped me when there
were no more roads open for me. First, they helped me open a bank account and
now they have helped me build a house. I am ever grateful to them.[40]

When asked about how these women write letters and do all the paperwork
since they are not educated, Raha B said:

We have a very understanding master who teaches in the school, he writes all our
applications and letters, He is very patient, look at these letters, how beautifully
he writes. I asked him once to help but now he always comes to write for us.[41]

Apart from women-related issues, these women have also worked on various
development issues such as getting the road to the village constructed for
general public use, creation of drainage systems, fencing, construction of hospitals and toilets, implementation of water schemes, and so on, up-gradation
of schools up to the tenth standard. According to the local villagers, developmental work has considerably improved after women have been elected since
there has been a better flow of funds in the village because of their efforts.

More than the challenges of patriarchy in decision making, these women, like their male counterparts, often face challenges in the form of threats to their life from the militants. For instance, Malsooma Akhter (name changed) shared this:

> Some unknown gunmen forced our family to come out of the house. One gunman started beating me with an iron rod, we don't know who they were, but they asked me to resign or else they will kill me. But I did not resign and did not stop my work as the deputy sarpanch.[42]

Similarly, Raha B also mentioned that she received a letter from a militant group that demanded her to resign, but she refused and instead approached the police authorities. She added this:

> Earlier we had three female *panchs*, but one of the *panch* resigned since her relative belonged to a militant group and he had threatened her to leave the halqa.

Many women representatives in the panchayat halqas continue to face militant threats and some have died. For example, another woman panchayat member, was shot in the neck and head by suspected militants inside her house in Baramulla district in January 2013. Thankfully, she is alive, but was going through tremendous physical and emotional trauma. Similarly, Sabiya (name changed), a woman panchayat member from another block faces real challenges in discharging her duties. She has been threatened by unknown groups to resign, but she has refused to oblige and continues to work as the sarpanch.[43] The elected women representatives are seen as traitors by the resisters and militants. As some young resisters remarked, "Any Kashmiri performing duties for the Indian state in Kashmir is a traitor in our struggle for freedom." The elected women representatives in Panchayat often get stuck in the power struggle between the state and militants. However, they engage with this interplay of masculinities in different ways. Some women choose to comply with the demands of the militancy, while some continue to discharge their duties despite the threat to their lives and everyday challenges.

The case of the elected women representatives in the village panchayats indicates a few important things. First, that generalizing women's agency even at such a microlevel is futile, because women's choices are varied depending on their experiences. Some women reinforce patriarchy both at their homes and through their representation in the panchayats, while others proactively work for women-related issues. Second, within the contestation of two masculine projects–state on the one hand and militancy on the other hand, women are expected to make strong choices. Such choices depend on their respective circumstances, past experiences, and family situations.

Thirdly, despite the masculine domination in homes, panchayat systems, and armed resistance, women find creative ways to exercise their choices and interests. Even at the macro level, agency of women in the Kashmir conflict is complex and diverse. It cannot be analyzed through the oversimplified frames of victims, perpetrators, and actors. Although several images, symbols, narratives, and representations are created to limit their role and expectations, as the discussion in this chapter shows, women find different ways to exercise agency within the confines created by the masculine patriarchal projects. There are multiple ways in which they navigate the patriarchal structures, through exercising both complicit and subversive agency. As mentioned before, the study of women's agency is incomplete without taking into account the expectations of femininity that are drawn by the patriarchal structures of family, military, militancy, and the resistance movement itself. The engagement of women's agency with the interplay of masculinities facilitates highlighting the nuances and complexities of agency. There are significant dialectics between the experiences of men; their perception of masculinities and women's role and agency. This chapter has showed some ways in which stories about women's role in the conflict and resistance are told to reinforce patriarchal values. Furthermore, through multiple examples, it also showed how women engage with these stories and find empowering ways to navigate patriarchy (also by sometimes upholding it) in both the public and the private spheres, based on their respective vantage points.

REFERENCES

Agarwal, Amya. "Mothers Shaping Masculine Ideals of Mujahid in Kashmiri Resistance." *International feminist Journal of Politics*, Vol. 20, Issue, 4, 2018: 654–56.

Banerjee, Sikata. "Armed Masculinity, Hindu Nationalism and Female Political Participation in India: Heroic Mothers, Chaste Wives and Celibate Warriors" *International Feminist Journal of Politics*, Vol. 8, Issue 1, 2006: 62–83.

Bayard de Volo, Lorraine. "Drafting Motherhood: Maternal Imagery and Organizations in the United States and Nicaragua," in Lorentzen, L. and Turpin, J. (eds.), *The Women and War Reader.* New York: NYU Press, 1998.

Chatterjee, Partha. *The Nation and its Fragments.* Princeton, NJ: Princeton University Press, 1993.

Chatterji, Bankim Chandra. *Anandamath*, trans. Basanta Koomar Roy. New Delhi: Orient Paperbacks, 2006 (1882).

Chenoy, A. M., and Vanaik, A. "Promoting Peace, Security, and Conflict Resolution: Gender Balance in Decision Making," in Inger Skjelsbaek and Dan Smith (eds.), *Gender, Peace and Conflict.* London: Sage, 2001.

Elshtain, Jean Bethke. *Women And War*. New York: University of Chicago Press, 1987.

Fleschenberg, Andrea. "Asia's Women Politicians at the Top: Roaring Tigresses or Tame Kittens?" in Kazuki Iwanga (ed.) *Women Political Participation and Representation in Asia: Obstacles and Challenges*, Women and Politics in South Asia Series, No. 2, Denmark, NIAS, 2008.

Habib, Zamrud Anjum. *Prisoner No. 100: An Account of my Nights and Days in an Indian Prison*. New Delhi: Zubaan. 2011.

Hall, Lucy B., Weissman, Anna L., and Shepherd, Laura J. (eds.). *Troubling Motherhood: Maternality in Global Politics*, New York: Oxford University Press, 2020.

Jaleel, Muzamil. *People Unlike Us: The India That is Invisible*. New Delhi: Harper Collins, 2001.

Jamal, Arif. *Shadow War: The Untold Story of Jihad in Kashmir*, New Delhi: Vij Books, 2009.

"Kashmir's Iron Lady Parveena Ahangar on BBC List of 100 Most Inspiring Women." January 2019. Available at: https://www.kashmirindepth.com/kashmirs-iron-lady-parveena-ahanger-on-bbc-list-of-100-most-inspiring-women/.

Khattak, Saba Gul. "Gendered and Violent: Inscribing the Military on the Nation State" in Hussain, Neelam, Mumtaz, S. and Saigol, R. (eds.), *Engendering the Nation State*, Lahore: Simorgh Women's Resource and Publication Centre, 1997.

Krystalli, Roxani. "Women, Peace, and Victimhood." *IPI Global Observatory*, 2020. Available at: https://theglobalobservatory.org/2020/10/women-peace-and-victimhood/ (Accessed on 18/01/2021).

Kumar, Ashwani. "Participation of Weaker Section in Panchayati Raj Institution of People in Jammu and Kashmir," in *International Journal of Innovative Research and Development*. Vol. 1, Issue 9, 2012. Available at: http://www.ijird.com/index.phd (Accessed on 10/06/2015).

Malik, Inshah. *Muslim Women, Agency, and Resistance Politics: The Case of Kashmir*. Switzerland: Palgrave Macmillan, 2019.

Manchanda, Rita. *Women, War, and Peace in South Asia: Beyond Victimhood to Agency*. New Delhi: Sage Publications, 2001.

Nandy, Ashis. *Exiled at Home*. New Delhi: Oxford University Press, 2005.

Neugebauer, Monica E. "Domestic Activism and Nationalist Struggle," in Turpin, J., and Lorentzen, L. (eds.), *The Women and War Reader*. New York: NYU Press, 1998.

"Painting that had the idea of Bharat Mata" available at: https://www.getbengal.com/details/painting-that-had-the-idea-of-bharat-mata (Accessed on 23/06/2021).

Parashar, Swati. "Gender, Jihad, and Jingoism: Women as Perpetrators, Planners and Patrons of Militancy in Kashmir." *Studies in Conflict and Terrorism*, Vol. 34, Issue 4, 2011: 295–317.

Parashar, Swati. *Women and Militant Wars: Politics of Injury*. London and New York: Routledge, 2014.

Peteet, Julie. "Women and The Palestenian Movement-No Going Back?" *Middle East Report*, January–February, 1986.

Pettman, Jan Jindy. *Worlding Women: A Feminist International Politics*. New York: Routledge, 1996.

Schofield, Victoria. *Kashmir in Conflict: India, Pakistan, and the Unending War*. New Delhi, Viva Books, 2004.

Sen, Geeti. "Iconising the Nation: Political Agendas." *India International Centre Quarterly*. Vol. 29, 2002: 154–75.

Sharma, Kanika. "Mother India: The Role of the Maternal Figure in Establishing Legal Subjectivity." *Law and Critique*. Vol. 29, Issue 1, 2018: 1–29.

Sobhrajani, Manisha. *The Land I Dream Of: The Story of Kashmir's Women*. New Delhi: Hachette India, 2014.

Sobhrajani, Manisha. "Women's Role in the Post-1989 Insurgency." *Faultlines*, Vol. 19, Issue 3, April 2008. http://www.satp.org/satporgtp/pulication/faultlines/Volume19/Article3.html (Accessed on 02/04/2013).

Utas, M. "Victimcy, Girlfiending, Soldiering: Tactic Agency in a Young Woman's Social Navigation of Liberian War Zone." *Anthropological Quarterly*. Vol. 78, Issue 2, 2005: 403–30.

Ul-Haq, Mahbub. *Human Development in South Asia 2000: The Gender Question*. New York: Oxford University Press, 2000.

Wagay, Muzamil, Sareem ul Abdullah, Abdul Majeed Tali, and Kahleeq Ahmed, "Women's Political Participation in District Kulgam (J&K): Opportunities and Challenges." Department of Social Work, University of Kashmir, 2015.

Young, Iris M. "The Logic of Masculinist Protection: Reflections on the Current Security State." *Journal of Women in Culture and Society*, Vol. 29, Issue.1. 2003:1–25.

NOTES

1. For theoretical conceptualizations on motherhood, see Lucy B. Hall, Anna L. Weissman, and Laura J. Shepherd (eds.) *Troubling Motherhood: Maternality in Global Politics*, New York: Oxford University Press, 2020; and for women's activism (also as mothers) in the South Asian conflicts and in Kashmir, see, Rita Manchanda, *Women, War, and Peace in South Asia: Beyond Victimhood to Agency*. New Delhi: Sage Publications, 2001; Manisha Sobhrajani, *The Land I Dream Of: The Story of Kashmir's Women*. New Delhi: Hachette India, 2014.

2. For more discussion on Young's logic of masculinist protection, see chapter 3, p. 49.

3. Even during the 2020–2021 COVID-19 crisis, some Hindu political leaders were seen worshipping "Maa corona" or" "Corona Devi."

4. Personal interview on 30/08/2014.

5. Personal interview on 01/09/2014.

6. Personal interview on 31/08/2014.

7. Interview on 22/06/2013.

8. Following is the translation of the poetry, also quoted in my previous article, "Mothers Shaping Masculine Ideals of Mujahid in the Kashmiri Resistance," *International Feminist Journal of Politics*, 2018:

Jaan Dedi Hui Uski Thi

Haq Toh Yeh hai ki Haqada na Hua

Aa rahi hai Pak Qabron Se

Shaheedon ki Nida

Ab Humare khoon se illal

(The sacrificed Life belong to him,

The graves of martyrs emit purity

His right is that his rights could not be fulfilled

Their voice will find its way through our blood)

9. Interview on 03/08/2015.
10. Personal interview on 30/07/2015.
11. Public Commission on Human Rights.
12. Bait-ul-Maal is a community-based structure through which people who are poor, destitute, orphans, or widows are provided assistance, be it monetary or other like clothing, food material, but mostly economic assistance is provided. The system is itself funded by the wealthy people in the community who provide alms, or any other help required. Its existence is rooted in Shariah, that is, Islamic jurisprudence.
13. Personal interview on 31/07/2015.
14. Personal interview on 31/07/2015.
15. Personal interview on 31/07/2015.
16. Personal interview on 01/09/2014.
17. Personal interview on 30/08/2014.
18. Personal interview on 29/08/2014.
19. Personal interview on 03/09/2014.
20. Jammu and Kashmir Coalition of Civil Society (JKCCS), *Half-widow, Half Wife?: Responding to Gendered Violence in Kashmir*, July 2011, p.6.
21. Islamic Human Rights Commission, "Half-Widows in Kashmir." 29 November 2011.
Available at: http://www.ihrc.org.uk/publications/briefings/9967-half-widows-in-kashmir (Accessed on 4/10/2014).
22. Ibid., p. 8.
23. Cited in Jammu and Kashmir Coalition of Civil Society (JKCCS), *Half-widow, Half Wife?: Responding to Gendered Violence in Kashmir*, July 2011, p. 6.
24. Personal interview on 31/07/2015.
25. Amnesty International, "A Lawless Law: Detentions Under Jammu &Kashmir Public Safety Act (PSA)," 2011.
26. JKCCS, op. cit., p. 17.

27. Personal interview on 05/09/2014.

28. Personal interview on 05/09/2014.

29. Personal interview on 05/09/2014.

30. Personal interview on 03/09/2014.

31. Personal interview on 03/09/2014.

32. Personal interview on 03/09/2014.

33. Personal interview on 03/09/2014.

34. For a discussion on Women's Participation in Halqa Panchayat in Kulgam, see; Muzamil Wagay, Sareem ul Abdullah, Abdul Majeed Tali, and Kahleeq Ahmed, "Women's Political Participation in District Kulgam (J&K): Opportunities and Challenges" Department of Social Work, University of Kashmir, 2015. Available at: https://www.academia.edu/7689236/Term_Paper_Womens_Political_Participation _in_District_Kulgam_J_and_K_Opportunities_and_Challenges (Accessed on 20/05/2015). For a discussion on Women's participation in halqa panchayat in Baramulla, see; Mehraj Lone, Problems of Women Panchayat Representatives in District Baramulla of J&K, in *Indian Streams Research Journal*, Vol.4 No.1, 2014, Available at: http://www.isrj.net (Accessed on 26/02/2015).

35. Personal interview on 02/08/2015.

36. Personal interview on 02/09/2014.

37. Personal interview on 04/09/2014.

38. Personal interview on 02/09/2014.

39. Personal interview on 06/09/2014.

40. Ibid.

41. Personal interview on 05/09/2014.

42. Personal interview on 06/09/2014.

43. As told in interview by the local inhabitants of villages in Baramulla district.

Chapter 6

Toward a More Nuanced Gender Approach to Studying Conflicts

By pulling together different threads of discussion in this book, I now aim to highlight some important lessons learned for the study of gender in conflicts. Through the case of the Kashmir conflict, this book has sought to show the significance of combining both critical masculinities and feminist lens in order to enhance our understanding of gender and agency in conflicts. Foregrounding the study of construction, performance, and interplay of masculinities is crucial to make sense of the agency of both men and women. This is because the expectations and roles of both men and women are informed by the context in which multiple masculinities are enacted and reproduced. So, to understand the context of the interplay of masculinities in the Kashmir valley, the book has focused on studying the contesting (military and militarized) masculinities of the state and non-state actors respectively in Kashmir. In this concluding chapter, I discuss three important areas in which the book has broadened the understanding of the gender dimension in conflict. The first is the importance and relevance of studying masculinities, especially in ongoing conflicts like Kashmir. Second, how foregrounding the interplay of masculinities helps in expanding our knowledge of agency of both men and women; and third, the employment of reflective field research methods that include a combination of decolonial, feminist, and ethnographic aspects enables a comprehensive understanding of gender in conflict. The discussion around these three areas will show how this book contributes toward developing a more nuanced gender approach to studying global south conflicts in general, and Kashmir in particular.

IMPORTANCE AND RELEVANCE OF STUDYING
MASCULINITIES IN THE KASHMIR CONFLICT

The absence of a detailed study on masculinities in the Kashmir conflict has been both an advantage and a disadvantage for the research entailed in this book. Due to the lack of developed theoretical parameters, I relied on the CSMM literature and research that was conducted in other sites and contexts. The illustrious work of critical masculinities scholars in other global north and south contexts, as discussed in this book, no doubt, has provided the much-needed ideational support; however, the out-of-context frameworks were not adequate to discuss the gendered realities in the Kashmir conflict. For instance, the previous discussions show how the cultural, historical, social, and religious aspects of the Kashmiri society have had an integral role in the construction of gender identities, behavior, and expectations; and these are best understood only through a context-specific analysis. In some ways though, the lack of a theoretical anchor also provided ample space (both theo-retically and also empirically) to develop frames that are unique to the local context of Kashmir. So, the analysis around the shaping of multiple mascu-linities (sometimes overlapping with other identities) was made possible by an in-depth study of the history of resistance, societal relations, and religious foundations of the Kashmir valley.

Coming to the question of significance and relevance of studying mas-culinities in conflict based on the explorations carried out in this book, the importance of studying masculinities in the Kashmir conflict is manifold. In line with the critical masculinities studies, first of all, the study of gender is incomplete without a detailed exploration of how gender influences men and masculinities. Mainstreaming gender often leads to a half-sided understand-ing of how gender operates. Focusing only on women's roles and partici-pation in conflicts leads to omission of the context in which they perform those roles and practices. Interjecting a masculinities standpoint, thus, helps in understanding the expectations and discourses around which women are involved in the conflict. The construction of masculinities and their projec-tion on men has a dialectical relationship with the positioning of women's roles and vice versa. Furthermore, in conflict situations, the gender identities are strongly affirmed and more direct (yet complex) due to militarization and armed resistance. Also, the public and private spheres are more fluid in conflicts, which leads to a stronger assertion and reassertion of gender roles and expectations. It is imperative to understand the gender ecosystem, and in this book, I have argued that adopting an inclusive gender approach helps us make holistic sense of performances, practices, and agency of multiple actors and stakeholders (both men and women).

Second, Kashmir provides a suitable example of the coexistence of multiple ways of performing manhood that forms a web of masculinities. Militarized men, demobilized former militants, civilian men, and male NGO workers and human rights activists all together represent a mosaic of masculinities. Due to the limitations of scope, however, I restricted my analysis in this book to the military and militarized masculinities of the Indian army and of the past and aspiring armed resisters. The interplay and contestation of these masculinities provides the context in which men enact their gender roles and women's expectations are framed.

To fully understand the idealized military masculinity of the state armed forces in Kashmir, I found it important to situate it in the Indian political context and show its intersections with the nationalist and religious discourses. For the same, I explained the ways in which military masculinity assumes different forms in India and sometimes intersects with the Hindu nationalist imaginations. Furthermore, the state military practices reflected in the counterinsurgency operations in the present Kashmir are influenced by the dominant Hindu nationalist discourse in mainland India. These have serious consequences for the valley, which is inhabited mainly by the Kashmiri Muslims. The challenges and threats thrown at the militants and resisters also form a major part of this idealized form of military masculinity and are visible in slogans, counter-graffiti, and engravings on the hills. Apart from the nationalist and religious intersections, I also explored the construction of the ideal military masculinity both in terms of traits and as a legitimizing strategy in Kashmir through different indicators such as physical and arms training methods and cinematic representations.

Through the interviews with the army personnel regarding their actual lived experiences, I have attempted to rethink the common association between military men and violence. In doing so, I ask questions like these: How do military men actually perceive their masculinity in relation to the idealized forms of military masculinity? And how can we rethink the concept of military masculinity through the actual lived experiences of the soldiers and army officers? The importance of research on state military masculinity lies in the finding that the constructed ideal forms do not always coincide with the actual lived experiences, perceptions, and practices of the army personnel. Some responses show that military men are often reflective and introspective about violent encounters. They feel emotional discomfort in the use of violence, and aggression is not always the best compass for military manhood. Instead of beginning with the projection of violence on military men, in this book I show that unpacking the process of masculinization is crucial to creating more empathetic pathways and frameworks for studying gender in conflicts. The study of military practices in this book also highlights the presence of contradictions and fluidity, and recognizing such nuances is significant in conceptualizing a positive engagement that can possibly carry the potential for social change.

The reflective assessment of men's identities and their contestation in this book next takes the form of the study of militancy masculinities. In doing so, I have looked at two significant periods in the Kashmiri resistance that shaped two different models of the masculinity of the Mujahid (militant warrior). The first was during the peak of armed resistance in the late 1980s and the second, during the phase of the "new" indigenous militancy after 2010. Through the narratives of former militants (both surrendered and ex-militants) and young men aspiring to be militants, I first explored the construction and meanings of manhood attached to being a militant in these different militancy phases. Both these models acted as significant platforms through which young men asserted their manhood in different political contexts, and religion has played a crucial role in the shaping of the Mujahid imaginaries of both these periods. However, such imaginaries are not as coherent and clear as they may seem. Through the study of both the state military and nonstate militarized masculinities, I show that the idealized forms of masculinities are dynamic and undergo changes over a period of time. Masculinity as a political mechanism or a legitimating strategy requires constant negotiation and renegotiation of masculine behavior and practices. Evidently, the shifts in the perceived masculine traits, practices, and strategies adopted by both the state military and the militancy movement suggest the dynamic nature of the masculinization process.

In the analysis of militarized men's identities, the demobilized masculinities of the former militants are also examined in the book. The challenges of reintegration into civilian life that entail economic, social, and identity-related factors are confronted by the former militants in creative ways. There is, however, a common tendency to associate men's vulnerabilities with loss of manhood, and I argue through the experiences of former militants there is a need to move beyond such superficial connections. This is because the "emasculation," "feminization," and "homosexualization" narratives overlook the ways in which they navigate their victimization and find different coping mechanisms to address their everyday problems. The physical (and sometimes sexual) violence experienced by the former militants and its coding as torture by the respondents are also important in assessing their perception of masculinities. In this regard, the research shows that male survivors of violence in Kashmir frequently use the word "torture" to narrate their experiences of physical and sexual violence. Although the confirmed cases of sexual violence are very few and it is difficult to validate these experiences, the coding of their experiences as torture has in a way provided them courage to engage with civil society bodies and form their own informal methods of empowerment.

I discuss more about the nuances of studying men's agency in the next section. But my main intention to enumerate the alternative ways to look at masculinities in Kashmir is to show that uncovering the construction and varied perceptions of manhood opens up new avenues to study the complex power relations in the conflict. The mere equation of masculinities with violence in conflicts has not been helpful in addressing the power dynamics and has in fact resulted in creating more binaries and essentialization of gender roles. A holistic analysis of gendered practices and behavior that reproduce power dynamics and contestation, thus, requires an assessment of how the men performing these practices also perceive manhood and how they maneuver spaces in relation to the gender expectations. Addressing the "man" question in the Kashmir conflict is still at the nascent stage in academic scholarship, and this book hopes to start conversations that do not simply view masculinities in the Kashmir conflict as men's violence but more as constructions that may not necessarily reflect the actual lived experiences of men. Finally, due to the strong presence of multiple ways of "doing male" in the Kashmir conflict, I argue that addressing these masculinities is not only significant and relevant in creating newer sites of knowledge production, but also enables highlighting tacit and invisible ways in which power operates.

BROADENING THE UNDERSTANDING OF AGENCY: A FOCUS ON EVERYDAY LIVED EXPERIENCES

In simple terms, the usage of agency in this book relates to the innumerable ways in which both men and women make sense of themselves, their identities, navigate the gender expectations, and negotiate spaces in their everyday lived realities. The foregrounding of interplay and contestation of military and militarized masculinities in the Kashmir conflict enables the expansion of our understanding of agency of both men and women. Starting from how military men position their actual lived experiences in relation to the idealized forms of masculinity, to the avenues created by armed resistance for young men to assert their manhood, and the informal coping strategies employed by former militants to reintegrate into the civilian life—these instances of male agency become visible through a more careful engagement with masculinities in conflict. In doing so, rethinking masculinities by moving beyond its monolithic association with violence and viewing it as a political mechanism and strategy enables a more nuanced understanding of the agency of both state and nonstate actors.

It is equally important to rethink the conceptualization of male vulnerabilities and victimization mostly described as "loss of masculinity." The male survivors of different forms of violence, as discussed in this book, do not necessarily see their experiences as emasculating and feminizing. Despite the challenges they face, some have accepted the reconfiguration of gender roles at home and some even felt heroic about enduring and surviving the torture. In this context, I have also argued against the commonly used denotation of "emasculation" for the overall situation of men in Kashmir. Such generalizations tend to create false gender portrayals, essentialize men's roles in conflicts and deny the agency of both militarized and civilian men. As can be seen from the examples of former militants and male survivors of torture and violence, they have in unconscious ways adopted multiple strategies to navigate their experiences. Unlike other conflict-affected contexts, there are very few programs and spaces available to former militants that address their concerns, yet informally they get together with relatives and community members to share their experiences and stories. Sometimes their narrations act as significant catalysts for political mobilization of youth resisters. The male survivors of violence, despite the feelings of humiliation and shame, also exercise agency in their interaction with civil society bodies. They use strategies like discretionary disclosure and selective engagement with NGOs and other nonstate actors, which I have discussed in chapter 4. Their choices are shaped by the sociopolitical context and opportunity structures available at their disposal. Hence, the oversimplified rendering of male victimization as emasculation overlooks all the creative ways and details of agency exercised by the male survivors of violence.

The understanding of women's agency in the Kashmiri resistance also broadens when we study its engagement with masculinities and patriarchal politics. How women navigate patriarchal structures in the public sphere and everyday patriarchy in the private spheres opens up new conversations around their agency. Instead of merely focusing on their participation and activism in the resistance movement, I have explored how women's agency and position have a dialectical relationship with masculinity. As I have already mentioned, women's choices and practice performances do not operate in isolation from the masculinities discourses. In fact, the coding of masculine norms and their rhetoric creates the context of gender expectations for women in conflict and resistance. I demonstrated this by discussing the maternal symbols, frames, and discourse that are an integral part of both the state military institutions and the nonstate patriarchal projects. In doing so, I explored the Mother India narrative based on Hindu conceptualization of femininity, which is central to the masculine protectionist imaginaries of the state military. Similarly, the "kind," "sacrificing," and "grieving" maternal imageries have a strong presence in the Kashmiri resistance movement. Such framings are significant to not only confine femininity but also reinforce masculinity, and as a result, they reproduce the essentialized gender roles and expectations.

It is only after a detailed exploration of the context, imposed discourses of femininity, and storytelling narratives that we can truly understand how women creatively negotiate and claim their space. In the later part of chapter 5, I have looked at the different ways in which women exercise agency in Kashmir, and these are not necessarily subversive of patriarchy. For instance, women have played (and continue to play) an instrumental role in shaping and reinforcing militant masculinity through multiple resistance practices. It is also important to note that women's agency is complex and diverse in Kashmir, and it cannot be oversimplified through victim-perpetrators-actors frameworks that have been used before. Depending on their varied vantage points and personal experiences with patriarchy, women have made diverse choices and adopted creative ways to engage with patriarchy. Through the interviews of Haniya and Zoya, for instance, I have showed the uniqueness and peculiarity of their respective agency. Haniya's agency reflects both confrontation with patriarchy at home in her younger days, yet a strong reinforcement and affirmation of patriarchal values is visible in her role in the resistance movement of the 1980s. Through reflections on her Muslim identity, Haniya engaged with patriarchy, both in questioning and upholding it. Her agency, as I argued, is religious, whereby she adopted political Islam as a way to carve out the identity, rights, and involvement of women in the Kashmiri resistance. Women who joined her organization also found a legitimate avenue to be involved in the resistance movement in their own right as a woman and support violence. However, her narrative of the political Kashmiri-Muslim woman upheld and reproduced patriarchal values through the imposition of codes and behavior toward all Kashmiri women. On the other hand, I described Zoya's involvement in the resistance movement as hybrid that combines the fight against patriarchy along with the pro-freedom sentiments. She has been vocal about women-related issues such as dowry, domestic violence, and empowerment, alongside her proactive involvement in the resistance movement. Sometimes these two struggles clash, and Zoya clearly states her dissatisfaction with the treatment of women's issues by the separatist leaders in Kashmir. Her engagement and questioning of patriarchal values of the resistance movement in Kashmir is noteworthy and important, however, as she remarks her "priority is the pro-freedom struggle." Her agency is thus exercised through navigating the patriarchy entailed in the resistance movement while putting forth women's issues.

I have also discussed the experiences of wives of former militants, widows, and half-widows to understand how they grappled with the presence and absence of their husbands. The violent experiences, absence, and reintegration of the former militants have had a profound impact on women's roles in the domestic sphere. How women confront these challenges in creative ways is illustrated through their recorded responses. Similarly, interviews with the widows of Dardpora village and half-widows across various districts of the valley highlight the myriad choices that they make to deal with absences and liminalities. As an extended conversation, I also enumerated stories and experiences of elected women representatives of the village panchayat halqas that show the multiplicity of meanings attached to agency. Apart from exercising both complicit and subversive forms of agency, some of these women are caught between discharging their duties as *panch* and *sarpanch* (elected representatives) and receiving threats from the militants and resisters.

I have (hopefully) in this book, stressed the importance of studying gender as an inclusive category that influences both men and women. When the coding of masculine norms is uncovered, the otherwise overlooked nuances of agency of both men and women become visible. Through a better understanding of the context of gender expectations, the diversity of creative choices, suggestive of both conformity and subversion, can be found. The significance of studying the multiple ways of claiming spaces not only lies in broadening the study of agency but also enables a bottom-up conversation that is centered on the everyday lived realities of ordinary people. Another point that I think needs to be reemphasized is the interwoven nature of victimhood and agency. The study of agency, in this book, has attempted to weave victimhood and agency together instead of viewing them as binaries. The often-used phrase, "moving beyond victimhood to agency," in some of the existing feminist literature on Kashmir fails to capture the simultaneous struggles of the actors. In this regard, I have argued that there is no moment of change when victims become agents in Kashmir. They constantly navigate their identities as a victim and agent, which is amply substantiated through the case of different stakeholders like demobilized militarized men, wives of former militants, widows, and half-widows. I have further discussed the need to recognize the interwoven nature of agency and victimhood by discussing how the young resisters use victimhood as a powerful category for political mobilization and gaining international solidarity. Several examples of the online circulation of pictures, writings, and sharing of resonating experiences with other resisters, such as exchanges with Palestinian youth on social media platforms are discussed, which have played an important role in strengthening the international recognition of Kashmiri resistance movement. These examples show the need to revisit earlier (separate) understandings of victimhood and agency.

LESSONS FROM THE FIELD: LISTEN AND REFLECT

My field research experiences reflect best what Swati Parashar once said in a seminar on "the coloniality of research and the research backstage":

> Fieldwork is not generalizable. No manuals, no ethics guidelines prepares one for what unfolds. It is important to hold onto that uncertainty and to the subjective experiences of fieldwork.[1]

What resonates the most with the above lines is the uncertainty, the subjectivity, and the inability to generalize field research. From my own experience as an "outsider" to the Kashmir valley, I found that the most productive way to engage with the field was to respect, listen, and reflect. The field unfolds its truth and provides answers only when we let it speak. In my preliminary visits, I was deeply conditioned and trained to look for answers that I wanted to know. I read different books on qualitative research methods, only to find them inadequate in addressing context-specific research concerns. However, after several interactions with the local inhabitants and my research interlocutors, I soon realized that despite an in-depth reading on field research methods and secondary research on Kashmir, my knowledge base is severely limited. These reading materials definitely provided a basic outline of the context and methods available to the researcher, but the field had so much more to say and my questions looked unworthy of the experiences I heard. In most of my field visits, I recorded as much information as people were willing to share. Sometimes my questions were only a way to start a conversation, and I let the narratives flow, which became my most used research method. I went through the notes the same day after each field visit to journal the gender-related aspects of each interview, photograph, and any other material that I found.

The point that I wish to make through my personal experience is that fieldwork is a reflective exercise, where a researcher's job is to keep evolving both their research and themselves as researchers. The manuals and guidelines can equip a researcher to handle the initial inhibitions and familiarize themselves with field research and the context, especially in volatile conflict zones like Kashmir, but how the research is driven mostly depends on the researcher's discretion, choices, and of course, the accessibility. Due to the tense nature of conflict-affected societies, there are several uncertainties and blockages that a researcher is required to navigate. In the introductory chapter, I have already discussed the challenges and ethical dilemmas that were a part of the research entailed in this book. Constantly navigating information received and confronting setbacks is a part of field research that not only enhances research skills, but in my view also provides a space for self-introspection and evolution. There is little discussion on how researchers working especially in conflict-affected contexts can be profoundly impacted (mostly emotionally) by the fieldwork. To record painful stories and repeatedly read/listen to them is an emotionally challenging exercise, and more conversations around coping strategies for researchers need to be pursued. Some field research manuals regard empathy exercised by the researcher as a significant part of field research. However, as an outsider to the context, empathy (as it is generally used) may feel distant to the researcher and sometimes may also privilege the researcher as a "savior." I argue through my field-research experience that empathy can be a meaningful exercise if we move beyond its understanding as a researcher's prerogative and, instead, view it as a process of emotional osmosis/transformation for both the researcher, interviewee(s), and the research itself. Alongside, the positionality of the researcher is also crucial in understanding the power relations between the researcher and respondents and the answers are sometimes dependent on such power dynamics. As I had discussed in the first chapter, it was important to constantly reflect upon my political situatedness and multiple positionalities such as a woman, a non-Muslim, outsider and understand what each of these meant for the research process.

Apart from the imperativeness of reflexivity in field research, the use of alternative research tools also significantly aided in uncovering gender nuances in conflict-related research. As can be seen, I have relied on pictures, poetry on the graves, graffiti, slogans on army camps, documentaries, training methods, folk songs, and cinematic representations, especially in Bollywood movies. The subtle indicators in these alternative and eclectic research tools have been immensely helpful in uncovering the gendered nature of the conflict. Also, for an outside researcher, some of these representations, especially graffiti and slogans, are easily accessible research material to study the field. For example, multiple graffiti of Burhan's praise and glory in different villages were crucial in building my understanding of the new wave of militancy in Kashmir and the support it received from the people living in the villages.

Furthermore, it is important to raise three important points around addressing the coloniality of field research practices (from my own experience of conducting field research in Kashmir): First, a careful and conscious choice of vocabulary helps to some extent, in avoiding the reproduction of power relations between the researcher and respondents. For instance, the choice of words such as "interlocutors," "research partners," and "collaborators" instead of "subjects" is useful in highlighting the mutual process of knowledge production. Secondly, the labor of research brokers, local friends, and translators is an integral part of the fieldwork and should receive due recognition and acknowledgement. At the same time, however, the identities of both the respondents and the brokers must be protected. Third, the usage of the word "fieldwork" in academia itself needs to be revisited because it is so much more than just extracting information from the field. From a researcher's perspective (at least in my case), it is a process of knowing unknown people, understanding their lived experiences, and sometimes finding lifelong friendships and opportunities for self-evolution.

The research entailed in this book has sought to combine decolonial, feminist, and ethnographic research methods by taking inspiration from other field studies in conflict areas. The everyday lived realities of people are at the center of the research, and through this book, I have tried to show that gendered nuances can be best understood through a bottom-up conversation. A more people-centric approach has helped in understanding the tacit ways in which gender influences both men and women in conflict situations. Such an inclusive approach that includes multiple stakeholders can possibly show ways to bring more positive social changes. Lastly, despite my sincere effort at bringing the stories of my respondents closer to the reader, sometimes the incommensurability of language to capture the pain, loss, and trauma results in feelings getting lost in translation. Keeping this limitation in mind, I still hope that this book enables more conversations toward a more nuanced gender approach to studying conflict situations. I would end the book by emphasizing that getting too caught up in the binaries and sides in conflicts, often limits our ability to think of empathetic and people-centric approaches. To question the gendered nature of conflict, complex power relations and militarized violence of the concerned actors; there is a need to foreground the rich realm of everyday life in conflict settings. Studying gender and more particularly, masculinities in conflicts opens new pathways to start nuanced conversations around such lived experiences of multiple stakeholders in a conflict situation. Men embodying violent masculinities is a limited under-standing of conflicts, because they also embrace vulnerabilities and navigate their challenges with care amid the masculine environment and expectations. Taking into account, the fluidity within the practice of masculinities and the dialectics of such practices with femininities, helps provide a better under-standing of agency and of conflict itself.

NOTE

1. Swati Parashar speaking on the webinar, "The Coloniality of Research and the Research Backstage," organized by the Danish Institute for International Studies on 15.06.2021. Video available here: https://www.diis.dk/en/event/coloniality-of-research-and-spotlight-on-the-research-backstage (Accessed on 17/06/2021).

Bibliography

Aboim, Sofia. *Plural Masculinities: The Remaking of the Self in Private Life*. Farnham, UK: Ashgate, 2010.

Ackerly, B. A, Friedman, E.J, Menon, K., & Zalewski, M. "Research Ethics and Epistemic Oppression." *International Feminist Journal of Politics*. Vol. 22, No. 3, 2020: 309–11.

Agarwal, Amya. "Mothers Shaping Masculine Ideals of Mujahid in Kashmiri Resistance." *International feminist Journal of Politics.* Vol. 20, Issue 4, 2018: 654–56.

Ahmed, Mudasir. "Why Educated Kashmiri Youth Continue to Join Militancy," *The Wire*, October, 2018. Available at: https://thewire.in/politics/why-educated -kashmiri-youth-continue-to-join-militancy (Accessed on 04/06/2021).

Akbar, M. J. *Behind the Vale*. New Delhi: Roli Books, 2002.

Amar, Paul. "Middle East Masculinity Studies Discourses of 'Men in Crisis': Industries of Gender in Revolution". *Journal of Middle East Women's Studies*. Vol. 7, Issue 3, 2011:36–70.

Amin, Mudasir, and Majid, Iymon. "Politicising the Street: Graffiti in Kashmir." *Economic and Political Weekly.* Vol. 53, Issue 14, 2018.

Anand, Dibyesh. "Anxious Sexualities: Masculinities, Nationalism and Violence." *The British Journal of Politics and International Relations*. Vol. 9, Issue 2, 2007: 257–69. Available at: https://journals.sagepub.com/doi/full/10.1111/j.1467-856x .2007.00282.x.

Anand, Dibyesh. *Hindu Nationalism in India and the Politics of Fear*. London: Palgrave Macmillan, 2011.

Ba, I., and Bhopal, R. S. "Physical, Mental and Social Consequences in Civilians Who Have Experienced War-Related Sexual Violence: A Systematic Review (1981–2014)." *Public Health*, Vol. 142, 2017: 121–35.

Banerjee, Sikata. "Armed Masculinity, Hindu Nationalism and Female Political Participation in India: Heroic Mothers, Chaste Wives, and Celibate Warriors." *International Feminist Journal of Politics.* Vol. 8, Issue 1, 2006: 62–83.

Batool, Essar, and Rather, Natasha. "The Denial of Rape by Soldiers in Kashmir by the Likes of Shekhar Gupta Illustrates the Impunity Enjoyed by the Armed

Forces." *Caravan*. 2016. (Accessed on 09/06/2016). http://www.caravanmagazine .in/vantage/denial-rape-soldiers-kashmir-shekhar-gupta-impunity-armed-forces.

Baines, E. *Buried in the hearts: Women, Complex victimhood and the War in Northern Uganda*. Cambridge: Cambridge University Press, 2017.

Batool, Essar, and Rather, Natasha. "The Denial of Rape by Soldiers in Kashmir by the Likes of Shekhar Gupta Illustrates the Impunity Enjoyed by the Armed Forces." *Caravan*. 2016. (Accessed 09/06/2016). http://www.caravanmagazine.in/vantage/ denial-rape-soldiers-kashmir-shekhar-gupta-impunity-armed-forces.

Baweja, Harinder. "Kashmir: A Calculated Gamble." *India Today*. April 30, 1992.

Bayard de Volo, Lorraine. "Drafting Motherhood: Maternal Imagery and Organizations in the United States and Nicaragua," in Lorentzen, L. and Turpin, J. (eds.). *The Women and War Reader.* New York: NYU Press, 1998.

Bazaz, P. N. *The History of Struggle for Freedom in Kashmir*. Srinagar: Gulshan Books, 1954.

Beasely, Chrisitine. "Rethinking Hegemonic Masculinity in a Globalising World." *Men and Masculinities*. Vol. 11, Issue 1, 2008: 86–103.

Behera, Navnita. C. *Demystifying Kashmir*. Washington: The Brookings Institution, 2006.

Behera, Navnita C. *State, Identity & Violence: Jammu, Kashmir and Ladakh*. New Delhi: Manohar Publishers and Distributors, 2000.

Belkin, Aaron. *Bring Me Men: Military Masculinity and the Benign Façade of American Empire, 1898–2001.* New York: Columbia University Press, 2012.

Bhaduri, Aditi. 2006. "Inshallah, Kashmir will become Part of Pakistan: Interview, Asiya Andrabi." *Outlook*, 4 August, 2006. Available at: http://www.outlookindia .com/article.aspx?232194 (Accessed on 20/08/2014).

Bhayana, Arshiya. "Reintegrating Kashmir's Ex-Militants: An Examination of India's Surrender and Rehabilitation Policy." *ORF Issue Brief.* October, 2019. Available at: https://www.orfonline.org/research/reintegrating-kashmirs-ex-militants-an -examination-of-indias-surrender-and-rehabilitation-policy-56044/ (Accessed on 31/03/2021).

Bhutalia, Urvashi. (ed). *Speaking Peace: Women's Voices from Kashmir*. New Delhi: Kali for Women, 2002.

Björkdahl, A., and Selimovic, J. M. "Gendering Agency in Transitional Justice." *Security Dialogue.* Vol. 46, No. 2, 2015: 165–82.

Bucar, Elizabeth M. *Creative Conformity: The Feminist Politics of US Catholic and Iranian Shi'I Women*. Washington: Georgetown University Press, 2011.

Bukhari, Parvaiz. "Kashmir: India's Pyramid of Unchanging Policy Posture," *Conveyor.* Vol. 3 Issue 2, April 2011.

Bukhari, Shujaat. "Why the Death of Militant Burhan Wani Has Kashmiris Up in Arms?" *BBC India.* 2016. Available at: https://www.bbc.com/news/world-asia -india-36762043 (Accessed on 26/06/2021).

Bulmer, Sarah & Eichler, Maya. "Unmaking Militarized Masculinity: Veterans and the Project of Military-to-Civilian Transition." *Critical Military Studies*. Vol. 2, Issue 2, 2017:161–81.

Butler, Judith. *Gender Trouble: Feminism and the Subversion of Identity*. New York: Routledge, Chapman and Hall, Inc. 1999.

Chaffee, Lyman G. *Political Protests and Street Art: Popular Tools for Democratization in Hispanic Countries*. Westport. CT: Greenwood Press, 1993.

Chatterjee, Partha. *The Nation and its Fragments*. Princeton, NJ: Princeton University Press, 1993.

Chatterji, Bankim Chandra. *Anandamath*, trans. Basanta Koomar Roy. New Delhi: Orient Paperbacks, 2006 (1882).

Chenoy, A. M., and Vanaik, A. "Promoting Peace, Security, and Conflict Resolution: Gender Balance in Decision Making," in Inger Skjelsbaek and Dan Smith (eds.), *Gender, Peace and Conflict*. London: Sage, 2001.

Chengappa, Raj. "Spoils of Holding the Heights." *India Today*, August 6, 1999: 47–50.

Chiovenda, Andrea. *Crafting Masculine Selves: Culture, War, and Psychodynamics in Afghanistan*. Oxford: Oxford University Press, 2019.

Chynoweth, S. K., Buscher, D., Martin, S., and Zwi, A. B. "Characteristics and Impacts of Sexual Violence against Men and Boys in Conflict and Displacement: A Multicountry Exploratory Study." *Journal of Interpersonal Violence*. 2020: 1–32.

Cock, J. "Gun Violence and Masculinity in Contemporary South Africa," in Morrell R. (ed.), *Changing Men in Southern Africa*. Pietermaritzburg, South Africa: University of Natal Press, 2001: 43–55.

Cohn, Carol. "How Can She Claim Equal Rights When She Doesn't Have to Do as Many Push-Ups as I Do? The Framing of Men's Opposition to Women's Equality in the Military." *Men and Masculinities*. Vol. 3, Issue 2, 2000: 131–51.

Connell, R. W. *Masculinities*. Cambridge, UK: Polity Press, 1995.

Connell, R. W. & Messerschmidt, James. "Hegemonic Masculinity: Rethinking the Concept." *Gender and Society*. Issue 19, 2005: 829–59.

Demetriou, Demetrakis Z. "Connell's Concept of Hegemonic Masculinity: A Critique." *Theory and Society*. Vol. 30, Issue 3, 2001: 337–61.

Directorate of Rural Development Srinagar. Information also available at: http://drdk .nic.in/SRO%20211%20Name%20of%20Sarpanch%20&%20Panchs/SRO%20 211.htm (Accessed on 02/08/2015).

Dolan, Chris. "Collapsing Masculinities and Weak States: A Case Study of Northern Uganda," in Frances Cleaver (ed.) *Masculinities Matter! Men, Gender, and Development*. London: Zed Books, 2002.

Duncanson, Claire. "Hegemonic Masculinity and the Possibility of Change in Gender Relations." *Men and Masculinities*. Vol. 18, Issue 2, 2015: 231–48.

Duriesmith, David. *Masculinity and New War: The Gendered Dynamics of Contemporary Armed Conflict*. London: Routledge, 2019.

Duriesmith, David. "Hybrid Warriors and the Formation of New War Masculinities: A Case Study of Indonesian Foreign Fighters." *Journal of Security and Development*. Vol.7, Issue 1, 2018: 1–16.

Duriesmith, David, and Ismail N. H. "Militarized Masculinities Beyond Methodological Nationalism of an Indonesian Jihadi." *International Theory*. Issue 11, 2019: 139–59.

Edström, Jerker, and Dolan, Chris. "Breaking the spell of silence: Collective healing as activism amongst refugee male survivors of sexual violence in Uganda." *Journal of Refugee Studies.* Vol. 32, Issue 2, 2018: 175–96.

Elshtain, Jean Bethke. *Women And War*, New York: University of Chicago Press, 1987.

Enloe, Cynthia. *The Curious Feminist: Searching for Women in a New Age of Empire.* Berkeley: University of California Press, 2004.

Eriksson, Baaz, M., and Stern, M. *Sexual Violence as a Weapon of War? Perceptions, Prescriptions, Problems in the Congo and Beyond.* London: Zed Books, 2013.

Farman Ali, Rao. *Kashmir Under the Shadow of Gun: Making of Alfatah.* New Delhi: Uppal Publishing House, 2012.

Feron, Elise. *Wartime Sexual Violence Against Men: Masculinities and Power in Conflict Zones.* London: Rowman & Littlefield, 2018.

Fleschenberg, Andrea. "Asia's Women Politicians at the Top: Roaring Tigresses or Tame Kittens?" in Kazuki Iwanga (ed.) *Women Political Participation and Representation in Asia: Obstacles and Challenges.* Women and Politics in South Asia Series, No. 2, Denmark, NIAS, 2008.

Flood, Michael. "Between Men and Masculinity: An Assessment of the term 'Masculnity' in Recent Scholarship on Men." in Pearce, Sharyn and Muller, Vivienne (eds.) *Manning the next Millennium: Studies in Masculinities.* Perth: Black Swan, 2002.

FriÐriksdóttir, GuÐrún Sif. "Soldiering as an obstacle to Manhood? Masculinities and Ex-Combatants in Burundi." *Critical Military Studies.* Vol. 7, Issue. 1, 2018: 61–78.

Fujii, Lee Ann. "Shades of Truth and Lies: Interpreting Testimonies of War and Violence." *Journal of Peace Research.* Vol. 47, No. 2, 2010: 231–41.

Gardiner, Judith K. "Men, Masculinities, and Feminist Theory." Kimmel, Michael, Hearn, Jeff and Connell R. W. (eds.) *Handbook of Studies on Men & Masculinities.* Thousand Oaks, CA and London: Sage, 2005.

Ganguly, Sumit. "Explaining the Kashmir Insurgency: Political Mobilization and Institutional Decay." *International Security.* Vol. 21, Issue 2, 1996: 76–107.

Ganguly, Sumit, and Fidler, David. P. (eds.). *India and Counter Insurgency: Lessons Learned.* New York: Routledge, 2009.

Gockhami, Abdul Jabbar. *Politics of Plebiscite.* Srinagar: Gulshan Publishers, 2007.

Goldstein, Joshua S. *War and Gender: How Gender Shapes the War System and Vice Versa.* Cambridge: Cambridge University Press, 2001.

Gowen, Annie. "This Violent Militant was a Folk Hero on Social Media: Now his death has roiled Indian Kashmir." *The Washington Post.* July 2016. Available at: https://www.washingtonpost.com/news/worldviews/wp/2016/07/11/this-violent -militant-was-a-folk-hero-on-social-media-now-his-death-has-roiled-indian -kashmir/ (Accessed on 26/06/2021).

Gray, H., and Stern, M. "Risky Dis/entanglements: Torture and Sexual Violence in Conflict." *European Journal of International Relations.* Vol. 25, Issue 4, 2019: 1035–58.

Habib, Zamrud Anjum. *Prisoner No. 100: An Account of my Nights and Days in an Indian Prison.* New Delhi: Zubaan. 2011.

Habibullah, Wajahat. *My Kashmir: Conflict and the Prospects for Enduring Peace.* United States Institute for Peace Press, 2008.

Hall, Lucy B., Weissman, Anna L., and Shepherd, Laura J. (eds.). *Troubling Motherhood: Maternality in Global Politics,* New York: Oxford University Press, 2020.

Hamber, Brandon. "Masculinity and Transitional Justice: An Exploratory Essay." *The International Journal of Transitional Justice.* Vol.1, Issue 3, 2007: 375–90.

Handoo, Bilal. "Rebel Resurrection?" Available at *kashmirlife.net.* (Accessed on 07/08/2015).

Hansen, Thomas Blom. "Recuperating Masculinity: Hindu Nationalism, Violence and the Exorcism of the Muslim 'Other.'" *Critique of Anthropology.* Vol. 16, Issue 2, 1996: 137–72.

Hartwell, Fabian. "Burhan Wani and the Masculinities of the Indian State." *Journal of Extreme Anthropology.* Vol.1, Issue 3, 2017: 125–38.

Henry, M, Higate, P and Sanghera, G. "Positionality and Power: The Politics of Peacekeeping Research." *International Peacekeeping.* Vol.16, No.4, 2009: 467–82.

Hollander, Theo. "Men, Masculinities and the Demise of a State: Examining Masculinities in the Context of Economic, Political and Social Crisis in a Small Town in the Democratic Republic of the Congo." *Men and Masculinities.* Vol. 17, Issue 4, 2014: 417–39.

Hooper, Charlotte. *Manly States: Masculinities, International Relations and Gender Politics.* New York: Columbia University Press, 2001.

Husnain, Ghulam. "Ready For Jehad: First Hand Account from Pakistan on How the Proxy War Is Bred and Sustained." *Outlook.* September 25, 2000.

Jamal, Arif. *Shadow War: The Untold Story of Jihad in Kashmir.* New Delhi: Vij Books, 2009.

Jaleel, Muzamil. *People Unlike Us: The India That is Invisible.* New Delhi: Harper Collins, 2001.

Kak, Sanjay (ed.) *Witness/Kashmir 1986–2016. India:* Yarabal Press, 2017.

"Kashmir's Iron Lady Parveena Ahangar on BBC List of 100 Most Inspiring Women." January, 2019. Available at: https://www.kashmirindepth.com/kashmirs-iron-lady-parveena-ahanger-on-bbc-list-of-100-most-inspiring-women/.

Kasturi, Bhashyam. "The Indian Army's Experience of Counter Insurgency Operations in J & K" *Aakrosh,* April 29, 2012. Available at: http://aakrosh.sasfor.com/aakrosh/the-indian-armys-experience-of-counterinsurgency-operations-in-jk (Accessed on 02/04/2015).

Kasturi, Malvika, and Mekhola Gomes. "Debate: History, Historians, and the Many Ideas of India: A Reply to Shonaleekha Kaul." *The Wire.* August 28, 2020.

Kaul, Shonaleekha. *The Making of Early Kashmir: Landscape and Identity in the Rajatarangini.* New Delhi: Oxford University Press, 2018.

Kazi, S. *Between Democracy and Nation: Gender and Militarization in Kashmir.* New Delhi: Women Unlimited, 2009.

Khalidi, Omar. "Ethnic Group Recruitment in the Indian Army: The Contrasting Cases of Sikhs, Muslims, Gurkhas and Others." *Pacific Affairs*. Vol.74, Issue 4, Winter 2001–2002: 529–52.

Khan, Nyla Ali. *The Life of a Kashmiri Woman: Dialectic of Resistance and Accommodation*. New York: Palgrave Macmillan, 2014.

Khan, Rehman Hafizur. "Abdullah's Release and Re-arrest." *Pakistan Horizon*. Vol. 11, Issue 2, 1958: 99–109.

Khattak, Saba Gul. "Gendered and Violent: Inscribing the Military on the Nation State." in Hussain, Neelam, Mumtaz, S., and Saigol, R. (eds.), *Engendering the Nation State*, Lahore: Simorgh Women's Resource and Publication Centre, 1997.

Kimmel, Michael. "Integrating men into the curriculum." *Duke Journal of Gender, Law, and Policy* 4, 1997. Available at: http://www.law.duke.edu/journals/djglp/articles/gen4p181.html (Accessed on 08/10/2020).

KL News Network. "1975 Accord changed J& K's Special Status: Sajad Lone" *Kashmir Life*. March 27, 2019. Available at: https://kashmirlife.net/1975-accord-changed-jks-special-status-sajad-lone-205643/.

Kreft, Anne-Katherine, and Schulz, Philipp. "Beyond Passive Victims and Agentic Survivors: Responses to Conflict Related Sexual Violence." *E-International Relations*, 2021. Available at: https://www.e-ir.info/2021/04/03/beyond-passive-victims-and-agentic-survivors-responses-to-conflict-related-sexual-violence/ (Accessed on 06/04/21).

Krystalli, Roxani. "Women, Peace, and Victimhood." *IPI Global Observatory*, 2020. Available at: https://theglobalobservatory.org/2020/10/women-peace-and-victimhood/ (Accessed on 18/01/2021).

Kumar, Ashwani. "Participation of Weaker Section in Panchayati Raj Institution of People in Jammu and Kashmir," in *International Journal of Innovative Research and Development.* Vol. 1, Issue 9, 2012.

Leiby, Michele. "Digging in the Archives: The Promise and Perils of Primary Documents." *Politics & Society*. Vol. 37, No. 1, March 2009: 75–99.

Lone, Mehraj. Problems of Women Panchayat Representatives in District Baramulla of J&K, in *Indian Streams Research Journal*, Vol. 4, No. 1, 2014. Available at: http://www.isrj.net (Accessed on 26/02/2015).

Mahmood, Saba. "Feminist Theory, Embodiment and the Docile Agent: Some Reflections on the Egyptian Islamic Revival." *Cultural Anthropology.* Vol. 16, No. 2, (2001): 202–36.

Malik, Inshah. *Muslim Women, Agency, and Resistance Politics: The Case of Kashmir*. Switzerland: Palgrave Macmillan, 2019.

Manchanda, Rita. *Women, War and Peace in South Asia: Beyond Victimhood to Agency*. New Delhi: Sage Publications, 2001.

Mannergren-Selimovic, Johanna. "Gendered Silences in a Post-Conflict Societies: A Typology." *Peacebuilding*. Vol. 8, Issue 1, 2020: 1–15.

Maycock, Matthew. *Masculinity and Modern Slavery in Nepal: Transitions into Freedom*. London: Routledge, 2018.

Masood, Bashaarat. "Guns and Poses: The New Crop of Militants in Kashmir." *Indian Express*. July 26, 2015.

McClintock, Cynthia. "The Media and Redemocratization in Peru." *Studies in Latin America Popular Culture*. Issue 6, 1987.

McNay, L. *Gender and Agency. Reconfiguring the Subject in Feminist Social Theory*. Cambridge, UK: Polity Press, 2000.

Ministry of Home Affairs, Government of Jammu and Kashmir, Home Department, Rehabilitation Policy, Reference: Cabinet Decision No.32/3 dated 31.01.2004. Government Order No.Home☐55/H of 2004 Dated: 31.01.2004.

Moller, M. "Exploiting Patterns: A Critique of Hegemonic Masculinity." *Journal of Gender Studies*. Vol.16, 2007: 263–76.

Morgan, David. "Theatre of War: Combat, the Military and Masculinities," in Harry Brod and Michael Kaufman (eds.) *Theorizing Masculinities*. London: Sage, 1994.

Morgan, David. "Theatre of War: Combat, the Military and Masculinities" in Harry Brod and Michael Kaufman (eds.) *Theorizing Masculinities*. London: Sage, 1994.

Mushtaq, Samreen. "Opinion - The Gendered Face of Violence and Erasure in Kashmir." *E-International Relations*. July 2021. Available at: https://www.e-ir .info/2021/07/06/opinion-the-gendered-face-of-violence-and-erasure-in-kashmir/ (Accessed on 20/12/21.)

Myrttinen, Henri. "Death Becomes Him. The Hyper-Visibility of Martyrdom and Invisibility of the Wounded in the Iconography of Lebanese Militarised Masculinities" in Baker, Catherine (ed.) *Making War on Bodies: Militarisation, Aesthetics and Embodiment in International Politics*. Edinburgh, UK: Edinburgh University Press 2020.

Myrittinen, Henri. "Disarming Masculinities." *Women, Men, Peace and Security*, Issue 4, 2003. Available at: ms1.isn.ethz.ch/serviceengine/ . . . /06_Disarming+Ma sculinities.pdf (Accessed on 8/24/2013).

Myrttinen, Henri, Khattab, L., Naujoks, J. "Rethinking Hegemonic Masculinities in Conflict Affected Contexts." *Critical Military Studies*. Vol. 3, Issue 2, 2016: 103–19.

Nandy, Ashis. *Exiled at Home*. New Delhi: Oxford University Press, 2005.

Naqash, Rayan. "Writing on the Wall: In Kashmir Graffiti meets Counter-Graffiti." *Scroll.in*. 2016. Available at: https://scroll.in/magazine/816041/writing-on-the-wall -in-kashmir-graffiti-meets-counter-graffiti. (Accessed on 17/12/2020).

Neugebauer, Monica E. "Domestic Activism and Nationalist Struggle," in Turpin, J., and Lorentzen, L. (eds.), *The Women and War Reader*. New York: NYU Press, 1998.

Noorani, A. G. *A Constitutional History of Jammu and Kashmir*. New Delhi: Oxford University Press, 2011.

Obeng, Samuel Gyasi, and Hartford, Beverly. *Surviving through Obliqueness: Language of Politics in Emerging Democracies*. New York: Nova Science Publishers, 2002.

Obrock, Luther. "Landscape in its Place: The Imagination of Kashmir in Sanskrit and Beyond." *History and Theory*. Vol. 59. Issue 1, 2020: 156–64.

"Painting that had the idea of Bharat Mata" Available at: https://www.getbengal.com/ details/painting-that-had-the-idea-of-bharat-mata (Accessed on 23/06/2021).

Pandey, Geeta. "Taking the Jihad to Kashmir's Women," *BBC News.* 30 May 2006. Available at: http://news.bbc.co.uk/2/hi/south_asia/5028844.stm (Accessed on 15/06/2021).

Pandit, I. "The 'Israel Model': The Fragile Paradise of Kashmir Faces an Existential Threat." *Middle East Eye.* December 3, 2019.

Pandita, K. N. "Kashmir Question" in *Kashmir Herald,* Vol. 2, No. 9, February 2003.

Panwar, Preeti. "Cease Fire Operations, Haven't the Pak Rangers read "Islamabad Well Within Reach message on the milestone?" Available at: http://www.oneindia .com/india/haven-t-pak-rangers-read-islamabad-well-within-reach-message-on -milestone-1504095.html (Accessed on 29/08/2014).

Parashar, Swati. *Women and Militant Wars: Politics of Injury.* London and New York: Routledge, 2014.

Parashar, Swati. "Gender, Jihad and Jingoism: Women as Perpetrators, Planners, and Patrons of Militancy in Kashmir." *Studies in Conflict and Terrorism.* Vol. 34, Issue 4, 2011: 295–317.

Parashar, Swati. "Competing Masculinities, Militarization and the Conflict in Kashmir." *International Feminist Journal of Politics (IFJP).* Vol. 20, Issue 4, 2018: 663–65.

Parpart, Jane L., and Parashar, Swati (eds.). *Rethinking Silence, Voice, and Agency in Contested Gendered Terrains.* New York: Routledge, 2020.

Peteet, Julie. "Women and The Palestenian Movement-No Going Back?" *Middle East Report,* January–February, 1986.

Peterson, V. Spike. "Gendered Identities, Ideologies and Practices in the Context of War and Militarism," in Laura Sjoberg and Sandra Via (eds.), *Gender, War, and Militarism: Feminist Perspectives.* Santa Barbara, CA: Praeger, 2010.

Pettman, Jan Jindy. *Worlding Women: A Feminist International Politics.* New York: Routledge, 1996.

Porter, A. "What is Constructed can be Transformed: Masculinities in Post-Conflict Societies in Africa." *International Peacekeeping.* Vol. 20, Issue 4, 2013: 486–506.

Puri, Balraj. *Kashmir: Towards Insurgency.* New Delhi: Orient Longman, 1993.

Rai, Mridu. *Hindu Rulers, Muslim Subjects: Islam, Rights, and the History of Kashmir.* Princeton, NJ: Princeton University Press, 2004.

Ray, Ayesha. "Kashmiri Women and the Politics of Identity." *SHUR Final Conference on Human Rights.* Rome: Luiss University, 2009.

Saha, Abhishek. "'Burhan vs Modi': Video game in Kashmir Shows Wani fighting for 'Freedom.'" *Hindustan Times,* November 2016. Available at: https://www .hindustantimes.com/india-news/burhan-vs-modi-video-game-in-kashmir-shows -wani-fighting-for-freedom/story-bi2SzXhM2SsPj8PDiBDsRN.html (Accessed on 31/03/2021).

Schofield, Victoria. *Kashmir in Conflict: India, Pakistan, and the Unending War.* London and New York: I. B. Tauris, 2003.

Schulz, Philipp. *Male Survivors of Wartime Sexual Violence: Perspectives From Northern Uganda.* Oakland, California: University of California Press, 2020.

Schulz, Philipp. "Recognizing Research Participants' Fluid Positionalities in (Post-) Conflict Zones." *Qualitative Research.* 2020: 1–18.

Sen, Geeti. "Iconising the Nation: Political Agendas." *India International Centre Quarterly.* Vol. 29, 2002: 154–75.

Sharma, Kanika. "Mother India: The Role of the Maternal Figure in Establishing Legal Subjectivity." *Law and Critique.* Vol. 29, Issue 1, 2018: 1–29.

Shekhawat, Seema (ed.). *Female Combatants in Conflict and Peace: Challenging Gender in Violence and Post Conflict Reintegration.* New York: Palgrave Macmillan, 2015.

Shepherd, Laura J. "Sex, Security, and Superhero(in)es: From 1325 to 1820 and Beyond." *International Feminist Journal of Politics,* Vol. 13, No. 4, 2011: 504–21.

Shepherd, L aura J. (eds.) *Troubling Motherhood: Maternality in Global Politics,* New York: Oxford University Press. 2020.

Silva, Jani de. "Valour, Violence, and the Ethics of Struggle: Constructing Militant Masculinities in Sri Lanka." *South Asian History and Culture.* Vol. 5, Issue 4, 2014: 438–536.

Silva, Jani de. *Globalization, Terror and Shaming of the Nation: Constructing Local Masculinities in a Sri Lankan Village.* Crewe: Trafford, 2005.

Sivakumaran, S. "Sexual Violence against Men in Armed Conflict." *European Journal of International Law.* Vol. 18, Issue 2, 2007: 253–76.

Sjoberg, Laura. *Gender and International Security: Feminist Perspectives.* New York: Taylor and Francis e-library, 2009.

Sjoberg, Laura and Caron E. Gentry. *Mothers, Monsters, Whores: Women's Violence in Global Politics,* London and New York: Zed Books, 2007.

Sobhrajani, Manisha. *The Land I Dream Of: The Story of Kashmir's Women.* New Delhi: Hachette India, 2014.

Sobhrajani, Manisha. "Women's Role in the Post-1989 Insurgency." *Faultlines.* Vol. 19, Issue 3, April 2008. Available At: http://www.satp.org/satporgtp/pulication/faultlines/Volume19/Article3.htm (Accessed on 02/04/2013).

Subramanium, L. N. "CI Operations in Jammu & Kashmir." *Bharat Rakshak Monitor,* Vol. 3, Issue 2. September–October 2000. Also Available at: http://www.bharat-rakshak.com/MONITOR/ISSUE3-2/lns.html (Accessed on 17/03/2013).

Suman, Maj. Gen. Mrinal. "Women in the Armed Force: Misconceptions and Facts" *Indian Defence Review.* Vol. 25, Issue 1, Jan–Mar, 2010. Also Available at: http://www.indiandefencereview.com/interviews/women-in-the-armed-forces/ (Accessed on: 21/3/2015).

Swami, Praveen. "Figures Back Case for Army Rollback in Kashmir." *The Hindu,* October 28, 2011. Also available at: http://www.thehindu.com/news/national/article2574588.ece (Accessed on 3/21/2012).

The Jammu and Kashmir Panchayati Raj (Amendment) Bill, 2013. Available at: http://jklegislativecouncil.nic.in/Governor/Bill%20introduced%20in%20LC/B-7.pdf (Accessed on 12/06/2015).

Theidon, Kimberly. "Reconstructing Masculinities: The Disarmament, Demobilization and Reintegration of Former Combatants in Colombia." *Human Rights Quarterly.* Issue 31, 2009: 1–31.

Thorp. Robert. *Kashmir Misgovernment* (edited). Srinagar: Gulshan Publishers, 2011.

Tickner, J. Ann. *Gendering World Politics*. New York: Columbia University Press, 2001.

Touquet, H., and Schulz, P. "Navigating Vulnerabilities and Masculinities: How Gendered Contexts Shape the Agency of Male Sexual Violence survivors." *Security Dialogue* (2020). Available at: https://journals.sagepub.com/doi/full/10.1177/0967010620929176.

Touquet, H., Chynoweth, S., Martin, S., Reis, C., Myrttinen, H., Schulz, P., Turner, L., and Duriesmith, D. "From "It Rarely Happens to 'It's Worse for Men': Dispelling Misconceptions About Sexual Violence against Men and Boys in Conflict and Displacement." *Journal of Humanitarian Affairs*. Vol. 2, Issue. 3, 2021. Available at: https://www.manchesteropenhive.com/view/journals/jha/2/3/article-p25.xml (Accessed on 25/03/21).

Touquet, Heleen and Gorris, Ellen. "Out of the Shadows? The Inclusion of Men and Boys in Conceptualizations of Wartime Sexual Violence." *Reproductive Health Matters*. Vol. 24, Issue, 47, 2016: 36–46.

Ul-Haq, Mahbub. *Human Development in South Asia 2000: The Gender Question*. New York: Oxford University Press, 2000.

Utas, Mats. "Victimcy, Girlfiending, Soldiering: Tactic Agency in a Young Woman's Social Navigation of Liberian War Zone." *Anthropological Quarterly*, Vol. 78, Issue 2, 2005: 403–30.

Uzma, Falak. "Kashmir's Wave of Quality Militancy." *New Internationalist Blog*. Available at: http://newint. Org/blog/2015/08/11/Kashmir-armed-youth-challenge-india/ (Accessed on 12/08/2015).

UN Security Council Resolution 47. Available at: http://unscr.com/en/resolutions/doc/47 (Accessed on 30/03/21).

UN Department of Peacekeeping Operations, Disarmament, Demobilization and Reintegration of Ex-Combatants in a Peacekeeping Environment: Principles and Guidelines (1999), available at: https://peacekeeping.un.org/en/disarmament-demobilization-and-reintegration (Accessed on 01/04/2021).

Wagay, Muzamil, Sareem ul Abdullah, Abdul Majeed Tali and Kahleeq Ahmed, "Women's Political Participation in District Kulgam (J&K): Opportunities and Challenges" Department of Social Work, University of Kashmir, 2015.

Whitehead, Andrew. *A Mission in Kashmir*. London: Penguin Global, 2007.

Whitehead, Andrew. "Kashmir's Forgotten Women Militia." *The Wire*, 2017. Available at: https://thewire.in/gender/kashmir-women-militia.

Wicks, Stephen. *Warriors and Wildmen: Men, Masculinity, and Gender*. University of Virginia: Bergin & Garvey, 1996.

Wood, Elisabeth J. "The Ethical Challenges of Field Research in Conflict Zones." *Qualitative Sociology.* Vol. 29, 2006: 373–86.

Xaba, Thokozani. "Masculinity and its Malcontents: The Confrontation between 'Struggle Masculinity' and 'Post-Struggle Masculinity' (1990–1997)," in Robert Morell (ed.), *Changing Men in Southern Africa*. London: Zed Books, 2010.

Young, Iris M. "The Logic of Masculinist Protection: Reflections on the Current Security State." *Journal of Women in Culture and Society.* Vol. 29, Issue.1. 2003:1–25.

Yousaf, Farooq. *Pakistan, Regional Security and Conflict Resolution: The Pashtun Tribal Areas*. London: Routledge, 2020.

Zalewski, Marysia. "What's the Problem with the Concept of Military Masculinity." *Critical Military Studies*. Vol.3, Issue 2, 2017: 200–5.

MISCELLANEOUS SOURCES

Civil Society Reports

Amnesty International, "A Lawless Law: Detentions Under Jammu & Kashmir Public Safety Act (PSA)," 2011.

Islamic Human Rights Commission, "Half Widows in Kashmir," 29 November, 2011. Available at: http://www.ihrc.org.uk/publications/briefings/9967-half -widows-in-kashmir. (Accessed on 4/10/2014).

"Jammu and Kashmir Reports Highest Internet Shutdowns Since 2012, 9 out of 27 Reported in 2016 itself," *Indo-Asian News Service*, February 2017. Available at: https://www.india.com/technology/jammu-kashmir-reports-highest-internet -shutdowns-since-2012-9-out-of-27-reported-in-2016-itself-1822267/ (Accessed on 06/06/2021).

Jammu and Kashmir Coalition of Civil Society (JKCCS), *Half Widow, Half Wife?: Responding to Gendered Violence in Kashmir*, July 2011.

"State of Human Rights in Jammu and Kashmir 1990–2005," published by *Jammu and Kashmir Coalition of Civil Society (JKCCS)*, The Bund, Amrita Kadal, Srinagar, pp. 260–61.

Journalistic News Reports

"Women Soldiers of Assam Rifles Deployed in Kashmir for Security Operations," *Press Trust of India*, July 2021. Available at: https://www.ndtv.com/india-news /women-soldiers-of-assam-rifles-deployed-in-kashmir-to-help-in-security -operations-2477212 (Accessed on 20/12/2021).

"500 Militants Active in J&K: DGP" in *The Times of India*, 3 January 2011.

"1975 Accord changed J& K's Special Status: Sajad Lone" *Kashmir Life*. March 27, 2019. Available at: https://kashmirlife.net/1975-accord-changed-jks-special-status -sajad-lone-205643/ (Accessed on 24/08/2020).

"Crossing Line: Operation Owl," in *Outlook*, 25 September 2000.

"Fair Presence" in *Kashmir Life*, December 14, 2014. Also Available at: http://www .kashmirlife.net/fair-presence-issue39-vol06-69854/ (Accessed on 26/02/2015).

"Kashmir's Iron Lady Parveena Ahangar on BBC List of 100 most Inspiring Women," January, 2019. Available at: https://www.kashmirindepth.com/kashmirs -iron-lady-parveena-ahanger-on-bbc-list-of-100-most-inspiring-women/ (Accessed on 06/09/2020).

"Omar Objects Army Removes Slogan from Srinagar," *Indian Express,* Mon, June
    24, 2013. Available at: http://archive.indianexpress.com/news/omar-objects-army
    -removes-slogan-from-srinagar-mountain-face/1133001/ (Accessed on 7/07/2014).

Videos and Documentaries

"Exclusive Report from Corps Battle School, Sarol J&K where Army gets Training
    to fight Terrorists" *YouTube.* Available at: https://www.youtube.com/watch?v
    =jz5n4Xdr-tk (Accessed on 14/03/21).
Guerilla Training of Indian Army: Counter Insurgency Training at Corps Battle School,
    Available at: https://www.youtube.com/watch?v=z1w4QVE2SEk (Accessed on
    26/11/2018).
Jashn-e-Azadi, A Documentary Film, made by Sanjay Kak, Available at:
    https://www.youtube.com/watch?v=kJnwGEk1fzQ (Accessed on 20/11/2015).
Kashmir Aflame, A Documentary Film, made by Tariq Mehmood, Available at:
    http://jammukashmir.tv/player/Documentary/Kashmir-Aflame-by-Tariq-Mehmood
    -1992.html (Accessed on 10/01/2015).
Kashmir's Torture Trail, A Documentary Film, made by Jezza Neumann, Available at:
    http://truevisiontv.com/films/details/134/kashmirs-torture-trail   (Accessed   on
    19/10/2014).
"Rigorous Training of Indian Army" *YouTube,* Available at: https://www.youtube.com
    /watch?v=G3PRmckS6k4, (Accessed on 02/10/2014).
Ocean of Tears, a Documentary Film, made by Bilal Jan. Available at: https://www
    .youtube.com/watch?v=foe-6ePl75I (Accessed on 18/08/2015).
Swati Parashar speaking on the webinar "The Coloniality of Research and the
    Research Backstage" organized by the Danish Institute for International Studies
    on 15.06.2021. Video available here: https://www.diis.dk/en/event/coloniality-of
    -research-and-spotlight-on-the-research-backstage (Accessed on 17/06/2021).
Video showing the training "Soldiers Training in India," Available at: https://www
    .youtube.com/watch?v=AzvDfakP0ek (Accessed on 20/09/2014).

Website References and Social Media Sources

Best Proud Indian Army Slogans, Available at: http://bcbilli.com/best-proud-indian
    -army-slogans-makes-me-proud-to-be-an-indian/ (Accessed on 19/05/2014).
Facebook page of Armed Forces Officials Welfare Organization. Available at: https://
    www.facebook.com/afowosociety/ (Accessed on 14/03/2021).
Indian   Army   website: https://indianarmy.nic.in/Site/FormTemplete/
    frmTempSimple.aspx?MnId=HEPwWEmrREvm6FAQs8JeSg==&ParentID=e/
    J4wC4Y24PIM3XSMyQDWg (Accessed on 14/03/21).
esamskriti.com: The Essence of Indian Culture, Available at: http://www.esamskriti
    .com/photo-detail/Kargil-Memorial.aspx (Accessed on 05/06/2014).

Indian Rashtriya Rifles facebook page: https://www.facebook.com/rashtriyarifle (Accessed on 14/03/2021).

Website Electronic Intifada at http://electronicintifada.net/.

Website Palestine for Kashmir at http://palestineforkashmir.wordpress.com/.

Index

Abdullah, Farooq, 24
Aboim, Sofia, 30
AFSPA. *See* Armed Forces Special
   Powers Act
agency: complexity of, 4, 37; as
   complicit, 112–15; after death, 81;
   freedom with, 117; gender and,
   1–13, 127; masculinities and, 127;
   meaning of, 3–4; of men, 86–90,
   131; narratives demonstrating, 100–
   101; in patriarchy, 133; reintegration
   navigated with, 86; of representative,
   97, 117, 121; in resistance, 96; in
   silences, 88; as subversive, 112–15;
   trust in, 89; victimhood contrasted
   with, 2, 38, 104–5, 111, 134; after
   violence, 38; vulnerability contrasted
   with, 86–90; of wives, 105–11; of
   women, 3–4, 14–15, 95–96, 109,
   121–22, 132–33; of youth, 89
Ahangar, Parveena, 26
Algeria, 23
alternative research tools, 136
Amarnath Shrine Board, 26–27, 76
Anand, Dibyesh, 50
Anandmath (Chatterjee, B.), 98
apartheid, 83–84
APDP. *See* Association of Parents of
   Disappeared Persons

Armed Forces Special Powers Act
   (AFSPA), 56, 71
arrest, 23, 116
Article 370, 22, 27, 28, 51
Assam Rifles (paramilitary force), 46
Association for Prisoners of Kashmir
   Families, 116
Association of Parents of Disappeared
   Persons (APDP), 26, 109

Baaz, M., 36
Bait-ul-maal (assistance system),
   107, 124n12
Bakshi, Ghulam Mahmad, 23
Banerjee, Sikata, 95, 99
Bayard de Volo, Lorraine, 98
Beaseley, Chrisitine, 30
Behera, Navnita. C., 25
Bharat mata. See Mother India
Bharatmata (play), 98
Bhartiya Janata Party (BJP), 50
Bhat, Maqbool, 25
binary, 47, 48
biology, 47
Björkdahl, A., 4
BJP. *See* Bhartiya Janata Party
bodily capital, 83
body, 59, 80–81, 103
Bollywood. *See* movies

153

Gentry, C., 4
Gojri, Zoone, 21
Goldstein, Joshua S., 45
Gomes, Mekhola, 28
goodwill (*sadhbhawna*), 62
Gorris, E., 36
graffiti, 61–65, *78, 79*
grave, *105*
graveyard, *104*
Gray, H., 37
Guerrilla War (Guevara), 73
Guevara, Che, 73
guns, 60, 72–76

half-widows, 109–11, 116, 133–34
halqa. See representative
Handoo, Bilal, 77
Hansen, Thomas Blom, 51
heart, 62
Henry, M., 12
Higate, P., 12
Hinduism, 9, 20, 27, 50–53, 98–99, 129
Hindutva, 50–51, 56, 68n2
history, 13, 19–28
Holiday (movie), 52
Hollander, Theo, 30
honor, 82
Hooper, Charlotte, 45
human rights violations, 6, 71
hunger strike, 116
Husnain, Ghulam, 74
hyper-visibility, 80–81

ideal: in India, 50–54; masculinities
    as, 29–31, 43–54, 129; military
    representing, 54, 57–58; mother
    shaping, 103; in movies, 52; as
    protection, 50; religion shaping, 35
identity, 8; complexity of, 33; in field
    research, 10; gender in, 19; of India,
    27–28; masculinities with, 130;
    Muslim, 3, 24, 34, 96, 101, 112–15,
    133; narratives relating to, 44; as
    outsider, 11; performativity of, 19;
    religion shaping, 34

inadequacy, 72, 84, 86, 88
India: Article 370 abrogated by,
    27; Bakshi strengthening, 23;
    Hinduism in, 9; ideal in, 50–54;
    identity of, 27–28; Israel with, 56;
    masculinities in, 50–54; politics
    against, 72; religion in, 129. *See also*
    Mother India
Indian army, 31, 52–53, 55, 56
Indira-Sheikh accord, 23
in-laws, 111
insecurity, 86, 110
interviews, 5, 10–12, 103–4, 117
invisibility, 28
ISL. *See* Islamic Students League
Islam: ideal shaped by, 35; masculinities
    and, 34, 71, 79–80; multiplicity
    of, 34; patriarchy in, 114; politics
    guided by, 113; resistance
    reaffirmed by, 24, 35, 71. *See also*
    Congregation of Islam
Islamic Students League (ISL), 24
Ismail, N. H, 32–33
Israel, 56

Jamat-e-Islami. See
    Congregation of Islam
Jameel, Maryam, 113
Jammu & Kashmir (J&K), 22
Jammu & Kashmir Liberation Front
    (JKLF), 25
Jehan, Akbar, 21
J&K. *See* Jammu & Kashmir
JKLF. *See* Jammu & Kashmir
    Liberation Front

Kalhana (author), 27–28
Kashmir, 11, *104*, 107; Abid in,
    9; graffiti in, *78, 79*; men in,
    54–65; programs in, 88–89;
    Singh, G., acquiring, 20. *See also*
    Jammu & Kashmir; Pakistan
    administered Kashmir
Kashmiris Fight for Freedom (Saraf), 72
Kasturi, Malvika, 28

About the Author

Amya Agarwal is senior researcher at the Arnold-Bergstraesser-Institut, University of Freiburg and teaching fellow at the University College Freiburg. She is also an associate fellow at the Centre for Global Cooperation Research in Duisburg. Prior to her postdoctoral research, she worked as an assistant professor at the Jesus and Mary College, University of Delhi, and a guest faculty member at the South Asian University in the Department of International Relations. She received her PhD in 2017 from the Department of Political Science, University of Delhi. Her writings have appeared in *International Feminist Journal of Politics*, *Uluslararasi Iliskiler*, *E-International Relations*, and (forthcoming in) *International Studies Perspectives*.

www.ingramcontent.com/pod-product-compliance
Lightning Source LLC
Chambersburg PA
CBHW021819270326
41932CB00007B/250